ACKNOWLEDGEMENTS

All the members of the evaluation steering
committee have contributed a great deal but we
would like to underline the special support given
by the two professors, David Cox of Imperial
College and Gordon Trasler of Southampton
University.

Within the Young Offender Psychology Unit two
other people contributed essential computer
programming. Vivienne Bateman wrote two
programs: one to validate the conviction data; and
a second to make this data compatible with the
format of the data base. Sheila Speirs, senior
psychologist, wrote programs which validated the
data from trainees and from institutional records;
she was also responsible for the programs which
integrated the data into a single data base. Four
psychological assistants with the unit, George
Digby throughout and at different times Tina
Hamilton, Sharon Moorhouse and Sue Over, have
carried out much of the essential data collection
and coding. The authors have been aided
throughout, both in data collection and in the
coding, by many other colleagues to whom we would
like to express our thanks.

We gratefully acknowledge the helpful advice given
by colleagues within the Directorate of
Psychological Services, the Research and Planning
Unit and SIA, the computer bureau which handled
the data. We would like to single out our
colleague Mark Williams for providing much
perceptive criticism.

Other members of the Prison Department, the
Probation Department and the Statistical
Department aided the project in various ways. In

particular the Statistical Department provided much data, including the conviction data and the basic information for Chapter 7.

Finally, we would express our appreciation to the Wardens (now Governors) and their staff in all six of the institutions in which we worked.

HOME OFFICE

TOUGHER REGIMES IN DETENTION CENTRES

REPORT OF AN EVALUATION BY THE YOUNG OFFENDER
PSYCHOLOGY UNIT

By   David Thornton
      Len Curran
      David Grayson
      Vernon Holloway

Directorate of Psychological Services

Prison Department

LONDON

HER MAJESTY'S STATIONERY OFFICE

David Thornton is a senior psychologist in the
Young Offender Psychology Unit.

Len Curran is a senior psychologist in the Young
Offender Psychology Unit.

David Grayson is a senior psychologist based at
Hindley Youth Custody Centre.

Vernon Holloway is principal psychologist in
charge of the Young Offender Psychology Unit.

CONTENTS

Page

1.   INTRODUCTION

THE TOUGHER REGIMES PILOT PROJECT

1.1 The 1979 Conservative Party manifesto
promised that 'in certain detention centres we
will experiment with a tougher regime as a short
sharp shock for young criminals'. In due course
the Home Secretary announced to the Conservative
Party Conference (October 1979) that the
experiment was to begin at two detention centres:
a senior centre at New Hall in Yorkshire, and a
junior centre at Send in Surrey. He described the
new rigorous regime in the following terms:-

> .... life will be conducted at a brisk tempo.
> Much greater emphasis will be put on hard and
> constructive activities, on discipline and
> tidiness, on self respect and respect for
> those in authority. We will introduce on a
> regular basis drill, parades and inspections.
> Offenders will have to earn their limited
> privileges by good behaviour ...... these
> will be no holiday camps and I sincerely hope
> that those who attend them will not ever want
> to go back there.

1.2 It was decided at an early stage that the
pilot project should be established within
existing legislation and that there should be no
positive selection of offenders by reference to
offence type or personal characteristics. All
offenders in the appropriate age group (17 and
under 21 for New Hall, and 14 and under 17 for
Send) who received detention centre sentences in
the committal areas of the two centres would be
subject to the new regime, except those receiving
more than the three months minimum sentence (who
would be received by neighbouring detention
centres) or those judged by the establishment's
medical officer to be physically or mentally unfit

for the regime (they would be transferred
elsewhere). New Hall and Send were chosen as
fairly typical detention centres of a suitable
size serving large metropolitan areas and offering
a balance between north and south.

1.3 Before the new regimes could come into
existence, there was a preparatory period of about
six months which included detailed regime
planning, consultations with staff, some staff
training and the opportunity generally for those
who had to apply the pilot project to accustom
themselves to what was being asked of them: a
description of some of the features of this period
is included in the chapter on regimes. It
culminated with the issue of the Note of Guidance
to Staff (reproduced at Appendix A and discussed
in Chapter 3) and the commencement of the new
regime shortly afterwards in April 1980.

1.4 A further development when, in September 1981
in slightly modified form, tougher regimes were
also initiated at Haslar in Hampshire (a senior
centre) and at Foston Hall in Derbyshire (a junior
centre) is not covered in the present report (see
Note 1.2).

THE EVALUATION

The scope of the evaluation.
1.5 The primary purpose of the pilot project was
to 'assess whether spending a period of weeks in a
detention centre with a more rigorous and
demanding regime could effectively deter young
offenders from committing further offences'. To
this end a formal evaluation programme was set up.
The evaluation's scope was not however limited to
an examination of reconviction rates. The Note of
Guidance indicated that the programme was to
include a study of the composition and
characteristics of the centres' populations, a

description of the actual operation of the pilot
project regimes including the reactions of staff,
and an assessment of the effects on inmates both
while in custody and as reflected in reconviction
rates. In addition patterns of offending and
sentencing practice in the centres' committal
areas were to be examined.

The assignment
1.6 The evaluation programme was assigned to the
Prison Department's Young Offender Psychology
Unit, working in conjunction with the Home Office
Statistical Department. The Young Offender
Psychology Unit was responsible for describing the
new regimes and examining their effect on the
young offenders sent to them. In doing this it
drew upon the Prison Index to identify samples of
trainees and on the Offenders' Index to provide
for each trainee studied a record of criminal
convictions. Brief descriptions of the Prison
Index and the Offenders Index are given in Note
1.1 at the end of this chapter. In addition, the
Statistical Department analysed data regularly
collected by them in order to discover whether any
general deterrent effect could be discerned, and
also whether sentencing practice changed in any
way.

The steering committee
1.7 A steering committee was formed to oversee
the evaluation. The membership of this committee
included two prominent academics (D R Cox,
Professor of Statistics at Imperial College, and G
B Trasler, Professor of Psychology at the
University of Southampton). The steering
committee was chaired by the Head of P4 Division
(the Prison Department division responsible
generally for policy on the treatment of sentenced
young offenders and therefore specifically for
the planning and implementation of the pilot
project). Both the Young Offender Psychology Unit

and Statistical Department had representatives on
it and in addition there were representatives from
C1 Division (the Home Office division responsible
for criminal policy), the Home Office Research and
Planning Unit, the Probation Inspectorate, C6
Division (the Home Office division responsible for
probation services) and the Department of Health
and Social Security (which has responsibility for
the implementation of some of the criminal
disposals available for juvenile offenders
including some that are alternatives to detention
centre training). The steering committee met
first in June 1980[1] and from then on received
regular reports on the progress of the research
and suggested refinements and modifications both
in relation to the kinds of data to be collected
thereafter and the ways in which researchers
interpreted data.

The elements of the evaluation
1.8 The evaluation team undertook to cover
initially the characteristics of trainees being
received into six detention centres: the two which
were to implement the pilot project regime and
four others with which comparisons were to be
made. Details included such features as offending
history, institutional experience, and home
background. This provides a useful description of
the kinds of people being sent to detention
centres. More specifically, it was important to
determine whether the courts continued to send the
same sort of person to detention centre after the
project began and similarly it was necessary to

---

[1]
It will be seen that data collection was determined and
put into operation before the steering committee started
its formal meetings. The steering committee therefore was
not able to participate in shaping the initial phases.

identify any sources of bias which might affect
the comparisons to be made later when the results
were analysed. The results of collecting this
information can be found in Chapter 2.

1.9 It was decided that a detailed description
would be given of the operation of the pilot
project regimes. A number of methods were
employed. Two researchers were given the task of
observing all aspects of the regimes and they
visited the six centres, concentrating most of
their attention on the two pilot project centres.
Chapter 3 gives an historical account of the
development of detention centre regimes and goes
on to record the results of the researchers'
observations of the regime, the staff and the
trainees in Send and New Hall. In this chapter on
the regimes, and indeed in those parts of the
following chapters in which it is relevant, for
the purposes of evaluation the 'tougher' regime
has been taken as meaning a more rigorous and
demanding one, as specified in the Note of
Guidance to Staff.

1.10 Having become established at the two pilot
project establishments, the observers went on
specifically to survey the experience and
viewpoint of the staff. This they did a few
months after the start of the experiment,
discovering the early responses of the staff to
the change, and conducting a second survey 18
months later, by which time the regimes might be
said to have settled down. The results of these
two staff surveys are included in Chapter 4.

1.11 In addition to the regime observation, teams
from the Young Offender Psychology Unit, together
with other Directorate of Psychological Services
personnel, gathered questionnaire and other
material from the trainees about their experiences
in the establishments. This information was

collected from trainees at different stages in
their training and can be found in Chapter 5.

1.12 Chapter 6 reports the various analyses of the
data collected in relation to whether the trainees
have a further conviction recorded against them
within one year of discharge from their detention
centres. In this work an attempt has been made to
identify and control for any differences which
might be attributed to influences other than the
tougher regimes.

1.13 During the planning stages of the evaluation,
it was envisaged that, in addition to the further
conviction data for individual offenders, a sample
would be followed during the period of supervision
after release (see Annex F to the Note of Guidance
at Appendix A to this report). It was necessary
to discover whether youths discharged from
detention centres were given any special or
different kind of after-care attention simply
because they were part of an experiment or because
they had gone to the pilot project detention
centres. Also, it was hoped to obtain some
particular indication whether the pilot project
had had an effect on the attitudes or states of
mind of its trainees which had lasted into the
period after release. Some work was done on
devising appropriate questionnaires, and the
possible content of enquiries during after-care
was discussed with various interested parties.
These included representatives of both the
Probation Service and of the Social Services - the
latter, in the case of junior detention centres
only, were responsible for the supervision of
approximately half of those discharged. In the
event, however, the National Association of
Probation Officers advised their members not to
co-operate with this survey; it was decided not to
proceed any further. However, some comment was

obtained from the Probation Inspectorate which
provided reassurance on the first point that
trainees, during after-care, were not treated in
any substantial way differently because they were
part of the experiment (see Note 6.4 to
Chapter 6).

1.14 The analysis of the effect of the existence
of tougher regimes on crime rates with particular
reference to those in the catchment areas of the
two regimes, and a study of possible changes in
sentencing practice, are contained within
Chapter 7.

1.15 It can be seen then that an attempt has been
made to create a number of separate sources of
information from which conclusions can be drawn,
and that these form the bases for the different
chapters. Sometimes this separateness amounts to
complete independence. For example, information
from questionnaire material from inmates should
provide results independent of observers' comments
about inmate reactions. Sometimes the
separateness is less complete. For example, the
content of the interview responses on which the
staff survey is based must, in a number of ways,
have been conditioned by the familiarity and
confidence achieved between staff and the two
observers of the regimes.

1.16 Generally we have tried to limit the
conclusions at the end of each chapter to what can
be said as a result of the particular form of
enquiry to which that chapter has been devoted.
Sometimes reference to information in other
chapters has been used to help interpret the
findings. Chapter 8 records our overall
conclusions, drawing together the various separate
investigations covered in the preceding chapters.

1.17 A note is provided at 1.19 for those who wish
to understand the steps in this process more
closely.

NOTES TO CHAPTER 1

Note 1.1   The Prison Index and the Offenders Index

1.18 The Prison Index is a computer system
containing information on persons held in Prison
Department establishments in England and Wales.
For sentenced prisoners, the details recorded
include name, date of birth and sex of the inmate,
current establishment, type of custody,
differences associated with changes in type of
custody and discharge, length of sentence and
offence. Historical computer files are also kept
of prisoners received and of discharges. The
Offenders Index contains details of each occasion
on which a person has been convicted for a
standard list offence (broadly equivalent to
indictable offences) or dealt with for a breach of
a previous sentence (details of intermediate
committal proceedings and acquittals are not
recorded). This Index covers convictions in
England and Wales. The details recorded on it
include the name, date of birth and sex of the
offender, the offence committed, the date and
court of conviction and the sentence imposed.
Both of these Indexes are maintained by the
Statistical Department of the Home Office.

Note 1.2   The evaluation timetable

1.19 The three main elements in the progress of
the evaluation were as follows:

i.   The trainee samples used in the evaluation
      are explained in Chapter 2. 'Reception
      samples' were drawn in 1979 (prior to
      commencement of the pilot project) and in
      1980 a few months after the start of the
      pilot project. These two samples were each
      taken from six separate establishments.

Conviction information taken from the
Offenders Index is organized in relation to
discharges for total years. The trainees
discharged in 1979 had all been free (and
therefore at risk of conviction) for one year
by 31 December 1980 and the discharges for
1980 by 31 December 1981. Statistics
Department had completed the collation of the
last of this material by the autumn of 1982
and it was at this point, in October 1982,
that the evaluation team received all the
relevant conviction information (previous
convictions as well as further convictions)
in one single data extraction for the two
samples above.

ii. Teams of data collectors took information
about trainees from the six establishments in
September/October 1979 and June/July 1980.
Data were also collected from the two further
tougher centres (Foston Hall and Haslar) in
June 1981 prior to the commencement there of
the new regime, and from all eight
establishments in October 1981, but these are
not included in the present analyses because
further conviction information only became
available in the autumn of 1983. There were
other smaller collections of data at
different times. The two observers were
frequently present in New Hall and Send from
January 1980 through into 1981, collecting
the material for the regimes chapter. Their
work for the staff surveys was done late in
1980 and again in 1982.

iii. The conviction material made available in
October 1982 was coded for the computer by
the end of the year. Entering these data,
integrating them with the rest of the trainee
data, removing errors and validating the
total material took until June 1983. Most of
the computer analysis was completed during

the second half of 1983. Some further
analyses were advised by the steering
committee and these, together with the final
write up of the report, were completed in the
first half of 1984.

2.   THE TRAINEES

INTRODUCTION

2.1 This chapter describes the characteristics of
the trainees received into the centres under
study.   In addition to giving an overall
description of the trainees it examines whether
the various samples differed in some way which
might bias the comparisons which are described in
subsequent chapters.

NATURE OF THE DETENTION CENTRE POPULATION

2.2 The sentence of detention in a detention
centre was introduced by the Criminal Justice Act
1948.   During the period covered by this report
the relevant statutory provisions were contained
in the Criminal Justice Act 1961[1].   They enabled a
court to order an offender aged 14 but under 21 to
be detained in a detention centre, usually for
three months but in certain circumstances up to a
maximum of six months, in any case in which it had
power to pass a sentence of imprisonment, or would
have had such power but for the statutory
restrictions on the imprisonment of young
offenders.   An offender serving or who had served

---

[1]   Since 24 May 1983 the operative provisions have been those
in the Criminal Justice Act 1982, Part I of which
abolished the sentences of borstal training and
imprisonment for young offenders under the age of 21,
introduced the sentence of youth custody and provided for
a detention centre order minimum of three weeks and
maximum of four months. The Act restricts the power of
the court to impose youth custody and detention centre
orders to those cases where it believes that no other
method of dealing with the offenders is appropriate.

a sentence of imprisonment of not less than six months, or a sentence of borstal training, could not be sent to a detention centre unless the court was satisfied that there were special circumstances. The 1961 Act also made provision for the supervision of a person released from a detention centre.

2.3 An account of the historical background to the introduction of the detention centre sentence is contained in Section 2 of 'Detention Centres' (1970), a report of the Advisory Council on the Penal System. The sentence was introduced with an eye to the 'type of offender to whom it seems necessary to give a short but sharp reminder that he is getting into ways that will inevitably land him in disaster.' (Official Report (Commons) 1947 vol 444, col 2138). The 1978 edition of the Home Office handbook 'The Sentence of the Court' described detention centres as providing 'a custodial sentence for young male offenders for whom a period of more than six months' residential training is not judged necessary or justified by their offences, and for whom non-custodial measures such as fining or probation are not considered suitable'. It reminded courts that 'the regime is not suited to those who are handicapped physically or mentally' and that the regime was intended to be 'constructive with firm discipline and a strong emphasis on education'. The Advisory Council noted in their 1970 report that 'the sentence of detention in a detention centre has developed from being a special sentence designed for a limited category of young offenders into the standard, and potentially the sole, form of short-term custodial sentence for young offenders in general'. Section 9 of the 1970 report contains an examination of the arguments about the suitability of different sorts of offender for detention centres[2].

---

[2] The historical background is described more fully in Chapter 3.

2.4 Prison Statistics (1952 et seq.) give some
indication as to the actual kind of young offender
received into detention centres. In the early
years there was some fluctuation in the criminal
histories of those received into junior detention
centres (age 14 to 16). Since 1960, however, the
number of trainees with no previous convictions
has settled around 12% of receptions. The numbers
of those having previous experience of custody
(generally approved school) was as high as 25% in
the year the first detention centre opened (1952);
this reduced to about 6% of the receptions by the
end of the 1950's but later climbed again to
around 18%. The picture for senior trainees
appears markedly similar; after 1960 the number
with no previous convictions dropped slightly from
14% and stabilised at about 9-12% for nearly 20
years. Those with previous custodial history rose
towards 1970 but varied little beyond 14-16% of
receptions thereafter.

2.5 A limitation of these official statistics is
that the definition of 'custodial history' does
not take account of local authority residential
care which embraces the whole range of residential
provision for children in care. On 1 January 1971
approved school orders were replaced by care
orders and such children could be placed by the
local authority anywhere in the child care system.
Two unpublished surveys carried out by the Young
Offender Psychology Unit in the mid 1970s
(Fludger, 1976; 1977) indicated that a substantial
minority of detention centre trainees had
experienced this sort of institutional care.
Analysis of the population of two junior detention
centres in the south of England revealed that
nearly 40% had some sort of previous institutional
experience (ie had served an earlier detention
centre sentence or had been in local authority
residential care). The second survey, which
involved a sample of senior detention centre

trainees in the south east, suggested that a
little over 20% of them had some kind of
institutional experience. With regard to the
offences for which they were sentenced to
detention, prison statistics indicate that the
vast majority of junior and senior trainees, over
the years, were convicted of offences of burglary
or theft. Amongst juniors in recent years only
12% of the receptions have been convicted for
offences involving violence; for senior trainee
receptions the figures are higher (22% involving
offences against the person) but current offences
for violence are still very much in the minority.

2.6   The two Young Offender Psychology Unit
surveys found that a substantial proportion of
detention centre trainees had abnormal features in
their backgrounds such as heavy drinking, drug
taking, attempted suicide, or psychiatric
referral.   That the detention centre population is
unusual in more than its specifically criminal
behaviour is also indicated by personality
research with the Jesness Inventory (Jesness,
1966; Fisher, 1967; Davies, 1967; Mott, 1969;
Saunders and Davies, 1967).   Various groups of
incarcerated young offenders (approved school,
senior detention centre, and borstal samples) have
been found to differ from unselected comprehensive
school pupils in that some attitudes and values
are more common within the delinquent groups.

DESCRIPTION OF TRAINEES INVOLVED IN THE EVALUATION

2.7   A number of researchers have reported
regional variation in the kind of offender
received into detention centre (Grunhut, 1955;
Dunlop and McCabe, 1965; Shapland, 1969).
Consequently characterisations of the detention
centre population as a whole cannot necessarily be
applied to trainees received into the particular
detention centres involved in the evaluation

programme. This chapter presents a general
description of the samples of junior and senior
trainees studied in the evaluation.

METHODOLOGY

Samples

2.8 Data were collected on trainees in Send and
New Hall and the four comparison centres during a
baseline period (period I) and then again after
the regimes in Send and New Hall had been modified
(period II). Two different kinds of sample were
extracted: reception samples and occupation
samples. Period I reception samples consisted of
all those trainees recorded on the Prison Index
(see Note 1.1 at the end of the first chapter) as
having been received into the six detention
centres (Send, Eastwood Park, Campsfield House,
New Hall, Buckley Hall and Werrington House)
between 1 May 1979 and 12 October 1979. Period II
reception samples consisted of all those trainees
recorded as having been received into the six
centres between 1 May 1980 and 5 September 1980.
Period I occupation samples consisted of all those
trainees in the six centres when our interviewers
visited in autumn 1979 (the visits were either in
the last week of September or the first week of
October). Period II occupation samples consisted
of all those trainees in the six centres when our
interviewers visited in summer 1980 (visits were
at the end of June and the beginning of July). It
should be noted that all trainees in the
occupation samples were also in the reception
samples though the reverse was not true, and that
all the trainees in the period II samples had been
received after the implementation of the pilot
regimes at New Hall and Send. The reception
samples comprised about three thousand cases, and
the occupation samples about eight hundred cases.

Sources of Data

2.9 Four sources of data were used. These were:-

i. **The Offenders Index**
    This provided details of all convictions
    for standard list offences incurred by
    trainees in the reception samples (see
    Note 1.1 at the end of the first
    chapter).

ii. **Questionnaires**
    These were administered to small groups
    of trainees by Directorate of
    Psychological Services (DPS) staff. A
    few trainees known to be illiterate were
    excluded. The questionnaires provided
    information about trainees'
    personalities and about the occupational
    status of trainees and their parents.
    These questionnaires were administered
    only to trainees in the period II
    occupation samples.

iii. **Interviews**
    All trainees in the occupation samples
    from both periods were individually
    interviewed by DPS staff. These
    interviews provided some information
    about trainees' backgrounds (eg their
    experience of local authority
    residential care).

iv. **Routine documentation**
    DPS staff searched the records of
    discharged trainees from the period I
    and period II occupation samples for
    details of punishments incurred whilst
    at the centre. Other details to do with
    self injury in the centre and sick
    reporting were also abstracted.

2.10 It will be apparent that, except for conviction data, the main source of most of the information about the trainees was the trainees themselves. We have not made any check on the accuracy of the information given by the present samples of trainees. This means that some of the tables that follow should be regarded with caution. Our experience has been, however, that trainees are reasonably reliable informants.

2.11 Some further, unavoidable, complications with the data need to be noted. During the periods when the psychologists and their assistants visited the establishments to interview and administer questionnaires to the trainees, some of those recorded as being in the establishment were unavailable (typically these would be at a court, in hospital or receiving visits). Occasionally too, the routine documentation was unavailable. This could arise in a number of ways. For example in a few instances trainees had been reconvicted by the time the researchers arrived to collect the information. In these few cases the routine documentation was unavailable because it had been forwarded to the trainee's new establishment.

2.12 The effect of these complications has been to produce small variations in the sample numbers. These are the main reasons why the number of cases varies in the succeeding tables. A few other cases are lost due to clerical errors in the documentation or in coding the data for computer processing. An example of this sort of error is that occasionally current year is recorded or coded for the trainee's year of birth. The number of cases for which valid data were present (N) is recorded separately for each table.

RESULTS

Table 2.1: Occupation samples by age on sentence

	Junior occupation sample	Senior occupation sample
14 Years	22%	0%
15 Years	41%	0%
16 Years	37%	4%
17 Years	1%	37%
18 Years	0%	29%
19 Years	0%	22%
20 Years	0%	8%
N	478	330

2.13 Table 2.1 gives the age on sentence of
trainees in the occupation samples. There are in
these data, as in the prison department annual
statistics, some trainees who are recorded as
being 'out of age', ie a junior trainee may very
occasionally be held in a senior establishment
(provided he is over school age) and vice versa.
Amongst the junior trainees those in the 15 and 16
year old age bands are more common than 14 year
olds. At the other end of the age range 20 year
old offenders, though eligible for detention
centres orders, are rare.

Table 2.2: Reception samples by nature of convictions

Offence type[3]	Junior reception sample		Senior reception sample	
	Currently convicted	Currently or previously convicted	Currently convicted	Currently or previously convicted
Violence	13%	21%	17%	28%
Sex	1%	2%	1%	3%
Robbery	3%	6%	2%	4%
Criminal damage	8%	24%	5%	26%
Burglary	52%	73%	35%	66%
Theft	40%	71%	33%	71%
Fraud	3%	7%	4%	9%
Motor[4]	30%	45%	32%	51%
N	1986	1986	991	991

[3] The offence categories used in this report generally correspond to those used in Criminal Statistics England and Wales.

[4] In this table, motor offences (theft of motor vehicle, taking and driving away etc) are shown separately from the theft category.

2.14 Table 2.2 gives the proportion of trainees in
the reception sample who were either currently or
ever (ie in either current or previous
convictions) convicted for various types of
offence.

2.15 Approximately one-fifth of the senior
trainees and less than a sixth of the juniors are
currently convicted for such things as violence,
sex and robbery. The majority are convicted for
burglary, theft and motor vehicle offences. The
numbers involved in robbery are tiny. A
substantial minority of offenders (between a fifth
and one third) have been convicted at some time
for violence against the person. Nevertheless,
again the most common offences are those involving
property. None of the offences against the person
were of the most serious kind (ie murder, wounding
with intent to cause grievous bodily harm etc).
This is unsurprising since these more serious
violent offences would generally incur a more
severe penalty than a detention centre order. The
sex offences were predominantly for sexual
assaults on an adult female victim (rape, indecent
assault[5]) in the case of the junior trainees or
for sexual intercourse with an under-age partner
in the case of the senior trainees.

2.16 Table 2.3 displays the number of previous
convictions incurred by trainees. In reading this
table it should be noted that what is counted is
the number of separate occasions on which the
trainee has been convicted. Since a trainee may
have been convicted for several offences on the

---

[5] Our data do not allow us to distinguish between rape and
indecent assault. It is very rare however for an offender
convicted of rape to be sent to a detention centre (Prison
Statistics, England and Wales).

same occasion it is quite possible for an individual with, say, three previous convictions to have actually been convicted for, say, thirty offences.

Table 2.3: Reception samples by number of previous convictions

Number of convictions	None	1-2	3-4	5-6	7 or more	N
Junior sample	21%	30%	25%	11%	13%	1986
Senior sample	10%	29%	28%	19%	14%	991

2.17 Just over half the junior trainees but only 39% of the seniors had been convicted on fewer than three occasions. This difference should not be taken as necessarily indicating that the junior trainees are in some way less criminally sophisticated than the seniors. The senior trainees (being older) have had more time in which to incur convictions. In addition, many of the junior trainees, but rather fewer of the senior trainees, who appear to be first offenders have had some institutional history which may have derived from difficult or anti-social behaviour as children (ie before the age of criminal responsibility). Two-thirds of both senior and junior samples have either three or more previous convictions or previous institutional experience.

2.18 Table 2.4 shows the sentences imposed on trainees for the previous convictions. The most common previous disposals were supervision or probation orders, fines, attendance centre, discharges and care orders.

2.19 Clearly in many cases a detention centre order is made only after various non-custodial penalties have previously been incurred.

Table 2.4: Reception samples by previous disposals

Previous disposal	Junior sample	Senior sample
Probation order	N/A	14%
Supervision order	44%	37%
Care order	22%	15%
Fines	35%	63%
Other payments	1%	1%
Attendance centre	24%	30%
Community service order	N/A	10%
Detention centre	6%	6%
Absolute or conditional discharge	42%	42%
Suspended sentence	N/A	1%
N	1986	991

2.20 Table 2.5 summarises the institutional history of those trainees who were interviewed.

Table 2.5: Occupation samples by institutional history

Type of institution	Local authority residential care				Previous detention centre	
	None	Under 12 months	12 months or longer	N	At least one previous DC sentence	N
Junior sample	46%	27%	27%	466	7%	478
Senior sample	72%	9%	19%	328	7%	330

2.21 Just over half the junior trainees, but under a third of the seniors, have previously been in some form of local authority residential care. Very few of the trainees have served a previous detention centre sentence. Taken together these observations suggest that the seniors are not just juniors a few years on but at least partially a different stream of people who first get into trouble later.

2.22 Table 2.6 indicates the proportion of trainees who report self-injury attempts, contact with a psychiatrist or a psychologist[6], or absconding (predominantly from local authority residential care).

---

[6] Predominantly child guidance since referrals on remand were excluded.

Table 2.6: Occupation samples by abnormal features

	Self-injury attempts		Psychiatric contact		Absconding		
	Per-cent any	N	Per-cent any	N	Once only	Re-peated	N
Junior population sample	11%	466	41%	466	8%	24%	466
Senior population sample	7%	327	18%	327	7%	6%	327

2.23 Nearly half the juniors have had some previous contact with a psychiatrist or a psychologist, compared with only one in five of the seniors. Similarly, about a quarter of the junior trainees report repeatedly absconding in contrast to about one in twenty of the seniors. The difference between juniors and seniors is less dramatic for reported self-injury although the frequency of this is still higher for the juniors. In interpreting these figures it is important to bear in mind the different opportunities that the juniors and seniors have had to accrue these 'abnormal' features. The senior trainees will have had more opportunity to injure themselves deliberately simply by virtue of being older. On the other hand, since substantially more of the juniors have been in local authority residential care, they have had more opportunity to abscond.

Table 2.7 Personality data for period II occupation samples

	Junior DC trainees		
	Mean	Standard deviation	N
B (Belief in human benevolence)[8]	15.5	5.1	285
P (Psychoticism) (Toughmindedness)[9]	6.5	3.7	283
E (Extraversion)[9]	14.4	3.9	"
N (Neuroticism) (Emotionality)[9]	12.4	4.7	"
L (Lie) (Response bias)[9]	7.3	4.0	"
I (Impulsiveness)[10]	13.9	4.3	282
V (Venturesomeness)[10]	9.6	3.9	282

[8] A low literacy version of the scale developed reliability (Cronbach's alpha coefficient) of 0.8.

[9] From the Eysenck Personality Questionnaire test constructors the adult version of this seniors. The results for normal samples are

[10] From Eysenck and McGurk (1980).

Senior DC trainees			Male normals (Age 16–19)		
Mean	Standard deviation	N	Mean	Standard deviation	N
14.7	5.0	165	–	–	–
7.0	3.9	163	4.6	3.3	540
15.4	3.7	"	14.5	4.3	540
12.1	4.7	"	10.7	5.1	540
7.2	4.1	"	6.1	3.8	563
14.2	4.5	"	–	–	
10.3	3.2	"	–	–	

by Thornton and Kline (1982). It has a

(Eysenck and Eysenck, 1975). On the advice of the
questionnaire was used for both juniors and
taken from the manual.

2.24 That these figures do not necessarily indicate that the juniors are a more 'disturbed' population than the seniors is confirmed by the personality data (Table 2.7)[7]. Significant differences are found only for two scales:- extraversion and venturesomeness. The junior trainees scored as being on the average slightly less extravert and less adventurous. These differences may reflect differences in age since extraversion at least is known to increase during early adolescence (Eysenck and Eysenck, 1975).

2.25 The table also shows some personality data for male non-offenders of roughly similar age (16 to 19 year olds). Both detention centre groups score higher on P and N (about two-thirds of a standard deviation higher on P and about half a standard deviation higher on N). Thus both junior and senior trainee samples appear to contain a higher proportion of difficult, unhappy and emotional individuals than does the non-offender sample. There is, however, no suggestion that the junior sample is currently more disturbed than the senior sample.

2.26 Two measures of the trainees' ability were obtained from the interviews carried out on the occupation sample. As the first part of the interview procedure trainees were asked to respond to a set of questions typed on cards. The trainees had to read each item aloud before sorting it into one of two piles to indicate his response. The interviewers intervened and read items to the trainee if he appeared to be having difficulty. Those trainees who had the card-sort

---

[7] Personality data were available only for the period II occupation samples.

items read to them were then recorded as being
'unable to read'. This variable therefore has a
practical if 'rough and ready' quality to it in
that it is a direct test of the trainees' ability
to read, although the interviewer's decision about
when to intervene obviously imports a subjective
element. A surprisingly large number of the
trainees were able to read - nearly nine-tenths of
both junior and senior samples (87% of 466 juniors
and 88% of 327 seniors). Following the card-sort
task, the trainees were given the similarities
test from the Wechsler intelligence scale[11]. The
average scores of both junior and senior trainees,
were similar to the average scores of similar aged
normal subjects as given in the manual (for
juniors raw score M=12.0, SD=3.6; for seniors raw
score M=12.4, SD=4.6; Ns of 465 and 327
respectively).

2.27 Those trainees in the period II occupation
samples were asked to describe their parents'
jobs. Table 2.8 categorises the jobs of those
parents who were described as being in paid
employment.

2.28 It is striking that the reported job level of
the fathers falls mainly in the lesser white-
collar, supervisory or semi-skilled groups rather
than in the unskilled category. The reported
occupational level of the working mothers is
somewhat lower than that of the fathers, except
for the professional/managerial group where the
proportions are the same. This may reflect the
fact that nearly half those mothers who were in
paid employment had only part-time jobs (see table
2.9).

---

[11] This subtest has a reliability of over 0.8 and is highly
correlated with the overall Wechsler IQ (Wechsler, 1955).
It can thus be used to give some indication as to the
general intellectual level of groups of trainees.

Table 2.8: Occupation samples by reported job level of trainees' parents

	Father		Mother	
	Junior	Senior	Junior	Senior
Professional/ managerial	12%	7%	14%	5%
Lesser white collar, foreman, supervisor etc	55%	54%	31%	29%
Semi-skilled	22%	21%	28%	28%
Unskilled	10%	18%	27%	37%
N	229	136	164	92

Table 2.9: Occupation samples by mother's employment status

	Juniors	Seniors
Not in paid employment	38%	45%
Part-time	28%	21%
Full-time	35%	34%
N	276	177

2.29 Trainees were also asked about their own work experience. Virtually half the senior trainees were unemployed at the time of their arrest, about a quarter were in unskilled jobs, and most of the remainder were in semi-skilled occupations. A similar breakdown of junior trainees' work experience was not attempted since the majority of

junior trainees were either still of school age or
would only just have left school.

2.30 The interviewers were asked to ascribe some
ethnic status to the trainees on the basis of
their appearance. This is an obviously crude
estimation of the trainees' ethnic background, but
we have information from other samples (outside
the evaluation) that such visual judgements of
ethnic status accord closely both with self-
ascribed ethnic status and parents' place of
birth. Fourteen percent of the juniors were
described as 'non-white' (N = 455) as compared to
5% of the senior trainees (N = 328). Three-
quarters of the junior non-white trainees were
described as black whereas only half the senior
non-white trainees were so described. These
differences between the junior and senior samples
reflect in some degree the ethnic composition of
their different catchment areas.

2.31 Information about trainees' height and build
was extracted from the routine documentation that
is completed on all trainees. The average height
for juniors was five foot six inches (SD = 3
inches; N = 452) and that for senior trainees was
five foot eight inches (SD = 3 inches; N = 325).
About a quarter of the trainees were described by
the reception officers as of small or slight build
(23% of 453 juniors; 29% of 327 seniors).

SUMMARY OF THE DESCRIPTIVE DATA ON DETENTION
CENTRE TRAINEES

2.32 The detention centre trainees in the samples
had most commonly been sentenced for non-violent
acquisitive offences, although around a quarter
had convictions for some kind of offence against
the person somewhere in their criminal record.
About half of the junior and over half the seniors
had been convicted on at least three previous

occasions. Very few trainees had served a
previous detention centre sentence though many had
experienced a variety of non-custodial disposals
and over half the junior trainees but only about a
quarter of the seniors had experienced local
authority residential care. There is a
corresponding difference between seniors and
juniors in the proportion who reported having
absconded: a third of the juniors but less than a
sixth of the seniors. A similar difference was
apparent in the percentage who reported previous
contact with a psychiatrist or psychologist:
virtually half the juniors as opposed to about a
fifth of the seniors. This result, too, probably
reflects the younger age at which the juniors
started getting into trouble rather than their
currently being a more disturbed population.
Personality data support this interpretation for
although they indicate that detention centres
contain a disproportionate number of
temperamentally difficult and unhappy individuals
in comparison with a sample of young male non-
offenders they give no indication of greater
disturbance amongst the juniors in comparison with
the seniors. The trainees' intelligence levels
appear to have been similar to that of the general
population, which is perhaps not surprising given
that the majority of the trainees appear to have
come from families of intermediate occupational
status (ie not from either professional/managerial
or unskilled backgrounds). Of those trainees who
were not at school about half were unemployed on
arrest and those who were in work were more likely
to be in unskilled or semi-skilled jobs than were
their fathers. About one in seven of the junior
sample was described as non-white, reflecting
Send's London catchment area. Only 5% of the
seniors were non-white.

CHECKING FOR BIASES IN THE SAMPLES

2.33 Evaluating the effectiveness of the pilot regimes at Send and New Hall depends on comparisons between the results observed for samples of trainees who experienced those new regimes with the results observed for those trainees who experienced the ordinary detention centre regimes. Differences in the composition of these samples might affect the result and so need to be taken into account if fair comparisons are to be made. This section seeks to identify these possible differences.

2.34 Previous research (eg Grunhut, 1955; Dunlop and McCabe, 1965; Shapland, 1969) together with official statistics has indicated both regional and temporal variation in the kind of offender received into detention centres. Thus we expected that the samples received into the different centres involved in the study would not be exactly equivalent and that the samples of offenders received in period I might differ in some respects from the samples drawn a year later during period II. The research design used in the evaluation was chosen because it allows us to estimate the distinctive effect of the pilot regimes in a way which is relatively impervious to these changes in the composition of the samples. As explained earlier we drew data from the pilot project centres (Send and New Hall) both before the new regimes were introduced (period I) and after the new regimes had been implemented (period II). In addition samples were taken from the comparison establishments in both these periods. This allows us to estimate the distinctive effects of the new regimes by contrasting the difference between period I and period II results for Send and New Hall (where the regime changed) with the difference between period I and period II results for the comparison establishments (where the regimes had not been deliberately modified). This estimate of the distinctive effects of the pilot regimes is not confounded either with constant differences between the centres in the kinds of trainee received (regional variation) or with differences between the two periods in the composition of the samples of trainees (temporal variation) so long as this occurs to the same degree at all the centres. The research design is however vulnerable to variation in the composition of the samples which is correlated with the introduction of the new regimes, ie a change in the composition of the samples which takes place in the pilot centres but does not take place in the comparison centres. This sort of change in the composition of our samples would bias the comparisons that we need to make in order to assess the distinctive effects of the new regimes. Accordingly we refer to it as sample bias.

2.35 Unfortunately it is not at all unlikely that such a subtle change in the kinds of offender being received into the various centres might have taken place. Introduction of the new regimes was accompanied by considerable publicity so magistrates in the Send and New Hall catchment areas will probably have been aware that from April 1980 'detention centre' meant 'tougher detention centre'. This may have affected their sentencing practice, leading them perhaps to give detention centre sentences to trainees who seemed to them particularly suited to a 'tough' regime. Although Home Office Circular 9/1980 explained the pilot project to the courts and requested them not to change their sentencing practice this does not itself guarantee that there were no such changes. Quite apart from deliberate reactions by magistrates to the advent of the new regimes, sample bias might also be produced by coincidental changes in the pattern of convictions in the catchment areas of Send and New Hall.

Coincidental changes of this kind might be
produced by such things as civil disturbances or
changes in police practice. Thus, despite our
choice of research design, sample bias is still
possible and it is therefore necessary to examine
the composition of the samples.

ANALYSIS OF THE COMPOSITION OF THE SAMPLES

2.36 A breakdown by sample of the data on trainee
characteristics is given below. (See Note 2.1 for
a discussion of how we have taken account of the
effect on samples of transfers on medical
grounds.) In order to facilitate interpretation
of these data an estimate of the sample bias
effect is also shown together with a test of its
statistical significance. These are displayed in
the two extreme right columns of the tables. The
estimate of sample bias is produced by subtracting
the weighted average change (between period I and
period II) at the comparison establishments from
the change shown at the pilot establishment[12]. In
interpreting these statistics there are several
points to take into account. In as much as we are
calculating a large number of statistical tests a
number of them are likely to reach conventional
statistical significance levels by chance. Thus a
few statistically significant results do not imply
that systematic sample bias is present. However,
regardless of whether sample bias has arisen
systematically or through chance processes it can
still bias later comparison if it is large enough.
Thus we consider not only all the instances where
sample bias is 'statistically significant' but
also cases where it is not statistically

---

[12] Both estimates of the size of sample bias and tests for
its statistical significance were obtained through the
ESTIMATE option of the GLM program of the SAS package (SAS
Institute, 1982). The required analyses is a three
(centres) by two (periods) analysis of variance with the
interaction term partitioned.

Table 2.10 Intake characteristics by sample for junior reception samples

Detention centre	Send		Eastwood Park		Campsfield		Sample bias	Sig of SB
Period Regime	I Ordinary	II Pilot	I Ordinary	II Ordinary	I Ordinary	II Ordinary		
Mean number of previous convictions	2.9	3.2	2.8	2.7	2.8	2.6	+0.5	0.02
Mean duration of conviction history (years)	1.6	1.6	1.8	1.6	1.6	1.6	+0.0	NS
Supervision experience	42%	43%	50%	43%	47%	42%	+7%	NS
Previous detention centre sentence	8%	9%	5%	5%	5%	3%	+2%	NS
Any conviction for violence offence triable summarily only	2%	6%	2%	2%	2%	2%	+4%	0.006

Any other violence conviction	25%	23%	19%	17%	23%	16%	+1%	NS
Any robbery conviction	8%	10%	4%	4%	5%	5%	+2%	NS
Any burglary conviction	69%	65%	74%	80%	73%	72%	-4%	NS
Any theft[13] conviction	67%	74%	74%	68%	72%	71%	+10%	0.022
Any fraud conviction	7%	5%	5%	7%	11%	9%	-2%	NS
Any criminal damage conviction	25%	18%	28%	24%	26%	22%	-3%	NS
Age on sentence (in years)	15.7	15.8	15.6	15.7	15.6	15.8	+0.0	NS
No of cases in sample	375	305	448	427	236	185		

13 Does not include motor theft. The offence variables shown in this table are those used in the analyses of reconviction reported in Chapter 6. Variables available, but not included here, tend to be either for the rarer or less serious types of offence. 'Summary violence' which might have been excluded on these grounds was retained because it showed sample bias and was associated with a raised risk of reconviction (especially for violence).

38

Table 2.11 Intake characteristics by sample for junior occupation samples

Detention centre	Send		Eastwood Park		Campsfield		Sample bias	Sig of SB
Period Regime	I Ordinary	II Pilot	I Ordinary	II Ordinary	I Ordinary	II Ordinary		
Mean height (in inches)	65.9	66.5	65.1	65.5	66.2	67.1	-0.0	NS
Skin colour (% white)	76%	72%	86%	93%	86%	89%	-8%	NS
Build (% slight)	16%	15%	31%	30%	17%	27%	-5%	NS
% Local authority residential care	49%	58%	59%	58%	42%	47%	+7%	NS

% Ever remanded in custody	34%	40%	23%	40%	11%	26%	-10%	NS
% Psychiatric contact	41%	60%	40%	33%	45%	31%	+30%	0.003
% Previous self-injury	7%	13%	4%	9%	21%	11%	+9%	NS
% History of absconding	34%	37%	36%	34%	26%	23%	+7%	NS
% Literate	82%	91%	81%	90%	95%	84%	+10%	NS
Mean similarities test score	12.6	11.7	11.1	11.8	13.4	11.6	-0.4	NS
No of cases in samples	70	107	46	130	38	62		

NB Exact sample sizes
fluctuate slightly from
one variable to the next

significant but is large enough potentially to
induce a non-trivial distortion of the later
analyses. The problem of 'significant' results
arising by chance where a large number of tests
are carried out has dissuaded us from offering any
substantial interpretation of the 'significant'
results.

2.37 Tables 2.10 and 2.11 show that statistically
significant sample bias was present in the junior
data for only four of the variables analysed: the
introduction of the pilot regime at Send was
associated with an increase in the average number
of previous convictions, an increase in the
percentage of trainees with summary convictions
for violence, an increase in the proportion of
trainees with convictions for theft, and an
increase in the proportion of trainees who
reported previously having had contact with a
psychiatrist or a psychologist (all these
increases being beyond those experienced in the
comparison centres).

2.38 Examination of those sample bias effects
which were not statistically significant discloses
that these effects were fairly small, the two
largest being a decrease (below the expected
figure) of ten percentage points in the proportion
of trainees who had been remanded in custody and a
similar sized increase in the proportion who were
literate. Neither of these effects are large
enough to have much influence on the results of
later analyses.

2.39 Analysis of the senior detention centre data
is complicated by changes in catchment areas which
took effect on 25 February 1980 in preparation for
the introduction of the new regime at New Hall.
It had been decided that the new regime should

apply only to trainees with three month sentences.
Since New Hall had previously taken some trainees
with six month sentences in addition to those with
three month sentences this necessitated a change
in the New Hall catchment area to enable it to
receive sufficient numbers of three month
trainees. This change in New Hall's catchment
area was part of wider catchment area changes for
the senior detention centre system which also
affected the comparison centres. (Send ceased to
receive trainees serving sentences over three
months but its catchment area was not affected.)

2.40 These catchment area changes raise a number
of problems for the evaluation. First, since
different kinds of trainees may be sentenced in
different areas some kind of sample bias might
have been introduced. Second, the extent to which
regional rivalries or antagonisms operated inside
the centres might have been altered. Third, the
quality of the environments, to which the trainees
discharged from a particular establishment return,
may have been altered (since areas vary in the
quality of the environment they provide). We have
employed three different methods to ameliorate the
effects of biases introduced by catchment area
changes. These are described in Note 2.2.

2.41 The following two tables show the breakdown
of trainee characteristics for the senior
detention centre data. The figures are adjusted
to reduce the effects of catchment area changes
using method B described in Note 2.2.

2.42 These tables reveal marginally significant
sample bias for two variables: criminal damage and
local authority residential care. The sample bias
arises not so much from changes at New Hall as
from changes at one of the comparison
establishments (Buckley Hall).

Table 2.12 Intake characteristics by sample for senior reception samples

Detention centre	New Hall		Buckley Hall		Werrington House		Sample bias	Sig of SB
Period	I	II	I	II	I	II		
Regime	Ordinary	Pilot	Ordinary	Ordinary	Ordinary	Ordinary		
Mean number of previous convictions	3.5	3.8	3.6	3.9	3.2	3.9	-0.2	NS
Mean duration of conviction history (years)	2.6	3.1	2.8	3.0	2.3	3.1	-0.0	NS
Supervision experience	41%	49%	53%	49%	50%	55%	+7%	NS
Previous detention centre sentence	5%	5%	7%	14%	4%	8%	-5%	NS
Any conviction for violence offence triable summarily only	7%	5%	7%	6%	6%	9%	-3%	NS

Any other violence conviction	25%	33%	27%	27%	24%	25%	+8%	NS
Any robbery conviction	5%	4%	3%	4%	3%	2%	-0%	NS
Any burglary conviction	73%	73%	66%	78%	70%	71%	-7%	NS
Any theft[13] conviction	75%	77%	66%	81%	75%	78%	-8%	NS
Any fraud conviction	8%	11%	15%	4%	9%	15%	+5%	NS
Any criminal damage conviction	26%	28%	28%	13%	29%	23%	+13%	0.094
No of cases in sample	116	186	153	56	53	84		

13 Does not include motor theft. The offence variables shown in this table are those used in the analyses of reconviction reported in Chapter 6. Variables available, but not included here, tend to be either for the rarer or less serious types of offence. 'Summary violence' which might have been excluded on these grounds was retained because it showed sample bias and was associated with a raised risk of reconviction (especially for violence).

Table 2.13 Intake characteristics by sample for senior occupation samples

Detention centre	New Hall		Buckley Hall		Werrington House		Sample bias	Sig of SB
Period	I	II	I	II	I	II		
Regime	Ordinary	Pilot	Ordinary	Ordinary	Ordinary	Ordinary		
Mean height (in inches)	67.5	67.1	68.9	68.1	67.9	68.0	-0.2	NS
Skin colour (% white)	89%	88%	94%	90%	100%	97%	+3%	NS
Build (% slight)	28%	29%	32%	28%	18%	27%	-2%	NS
% Local authority residential care	32%	19%	21%	51%	27%	20%	-24%	0.089

% Ever remanded in custody	31%	43%	40%	30%	40%	30%	+22%	NS
% Psychiatric contact	13%	22%	16%	38%	6%	17%	-8%	NS
% Previous self-injury	8%	8%	3%	6%	12%	6%	+3%	NS
% History of absconding	21%	19%	7%	11%	12%	5%	-1%	NS
% Literate	83%	87%	100%	98%	86%	87%	+6%	NS
Mean similarities test score	10.8	12.6	14.1	12.8	11.2	12.5	+1.9	NS
No of cases in samples	49	82	49	36	29	52		

2.43 Examination of those sample bias effects which were not statistically significant indicates that they were generally quite small. The one exception was for the percentage remanded in custody where the proportion in the New Hall period II sample was some 22 percentage points higher than expected.

IMPLICATIONS OF SAMPLE BIAS

2.44 Put somewhat crudely, the trainees received during the experimental period at Send were, taken as a whole, rather worse than might have been expected. That is, they were more often criminally sophisticated, violent, prone to theft, and 'disturbed'. Some of these characteristics are believed to be associated with a raised risk of reconviction. And this was true in the present sample for all except the indicator of 'disturbance' (psychiatric contact) as the following tables demonstrate.

TABLE 2.14 **Percentage reconvicted**[14] **by number of previous convictions for junior trainees**

Number of previous convictions

	0	1-2	3-4	5-6	7+
Percent reconvicted	35%	48%	60%	64%	70%
Number reconvicted	144	286	292	142	178
Number in category	415	593	490	223	225

[14] This is reconviction for any standard list offence within twelve months of release. For more details of the reconviction data see Chapter 6.

TABLE 2.15 **Percentage reconvicted**[14] **by conviction for violence triable summarily only for junior sample**

Convictions for violence triable summarily only

	None	Any
Percent reconvicted	53%	61%
Number reconvicted	1011	31
Number in category	1925	51

TABLE 2.16 **Percentage reconvicted**[14] **by convictions for theft for junior sample**

Convictions for theft

	None	Any
Percent reconvicted	44%	56%
Number reconvicted	253	789
Number in category	572	1404

TABLE 2.17 **Percentage reconvicted**[14] **by psychiatric contact for junior sample**

Psychiatric contact

	None	Any
Percent reconvicted	55%	56%
Number reconvicted	146	107
Number in category	267	192

2.45 Thus the introduction of the pilot regime at Send coincided with an unexpected increase in the average risk of reconviction of the trainees received. If not taken into account this sort of sample bias would lead us to give an unfairly negative picture of the effects of the pilot regime on reconviction rates.

2.46 In contrast the trainees received during the period II at New Hall might be regarded as having been rather better than would have been expected. That is, they had less often been in local authority residential care. The pattern of sample bias for New Hall is somewhat complicated however since there was an increase in the proportion of trainees who had been remanded in custody, which might be regarded as a deterioration. In addition the New Hall period II sample contained a disproportionate number of trainees convicted for criminal damage, which might also be regarded as a deterioration. The tables below show the actual relationship to reconviction of these trainees characteristics in the senior sample.

TABLE 2.18 **Percentage reconvicted**[14] **by local authority residential care for senior trainees**

Local authority residential care

	Never	At some time
Percent reconvicted	46%	53%
Number reconvicted	98	40
Number in category	213	75

TABLE 2.19 **Percentage reconvicted**[14] **by remand for senior trainees**

	Remanded in custody	
	Never	At some time
Percent reconvicted	45%	54%
Number reconvicted	87	57
Number in category	195	106

TABLE 2.20 **Percentage reconvicted**[14] **by criminal damage for senior trainees**

	Convicted for criminal damage	
	Never	At least once
Percent reconvicted	45%	52%
Number reconvicted	219	87
Number in category	482	166

2.47 Taking the results for the three variables together it is difficult to say whether the overall effect of sample bias at New Hall is either positive or negative. It looks as if the biases for the different trainee characteristics might just have cancelled each other out.

2.48 Fortunately the presence of sample bias does not render it impossible to make a fair comparison of the results obtained by the pilot regime with the results obtained by ordinary regimes. Statistical techniques exist which can remove the effect of sample biases for all measured characteristics. The proper application of these techniques is quite complicated though and as a result difficulties of interpretation can arise. The presence of significant sample bias means however that there is no alternative but to apply these more complex methods if we are to obtain a fair picture of the distinctive effects of the pilot regimes. Chapters 5 and 6 describe how this was done.

NOTES TO CHAPTER 2

Note 2.1 Effect of medical transfers

2.49 A small number of trainees received into the
pilot project centres were transferred to
comparison centres because they were considered,
on the basis of the reception examination by the
medical officer, to be physically or mentally
unfit for the pilot project regime (the relevant
guidance to medical officers is reproduced in
Appendix A paragraphs A.23 to A.30). During 1980
about 7% of receptions were transferred in this
way. The proportion was lower in subsequent
years.

2.50 The practice of medically transferring
trainees posed a problem because we had to
consider whether for the purpose of the evaluation
the transferred trainees should properly be
regarded as 'belonging to' the pilot project
centre to which they were orginally sent or the
comparison centre to which they were transferred.
Neither of these ways of categorising medical
transfers is entirely satisfactory. If they are
regarded as belonging to the comparison centre
then the non-random basis of the transfer process
(the fact that some kinds of trainees are more
likely than others to be transferred) will bias
the samples being compared, possibly creating
spurious differences in the results. On the other
hand if medical transfers are regarded as
belonging to the pilot project centre then this
may lead us to underestimate the size of the
differences between the regimes in the results
obtained. A compromise solution, dropping
medically transferred trainees from the analysis,
is also unsatisfactory since it too would bias the
samples to be compared.

2.51 The analyses reported in this and subsequent chapters are based on the second option (ie regarding transferred trainees as belonging to the pilot project centres). There were two reasons for preferring this option. First, the medical transfer procedure, with its consequence that a trainee judged unfit for the pilot project regime goes to an ordinary centre (unless he requires special medical facilities) and participates in the regime there to the extent considered appropriate by the medical officer, may be properly seen as an integral part of the pilot project. It was, indeed, covered in the Note of Guidance from the outset. Second, it was felt that the possibility of underestimating real differences was less unsatisfactory than that of creating spurious differences.

2.52 In practice it probably does not matter greatly which solution to the problem of medical transfers is adopted. The very small proportion of such trainees means that only a very marginal distortion is likely to have been involved.

Note 2.2 Effect of catchment area changes

2.53 This note describes the three methods used in the evaluation to allow for effects of biases introduced by the senior detention centre catchment area changes which took place on 25 February 1980. Method A, which is the most drastic, consists simply of restricting the sample to trainees sentenced by courts which had not been moved from one catchment area to another. This should provide a satisfactory control of the first and third problems mentioned in this chapter. It does not however satisfactorily take account of the second problem: eliminating from the analysis those individuals whose presence in the detention centre provoked regional antagonisms will not remove the effects these antagonisms will have had

on the other trainees. Unfortunately there is
nothing we can do about this problem except to
hope that the effects involved are small. Happily
there is some evidence that this is the case. Our
observer at New Hall (see Chapter 3) did not note
any regional antagonisms nor did staff offer this
as an explanation for fights or unruly behaviour
amongst New Hall trainees. Method A has one major
disadvantage. The proportion of trainees that
have to be dropped from the analysis amounts to
nearly a half of the senior detention centre
sample. Since the precision of our results
depends upon the size of the samples we are able
to analyse this is an important consideration.

2.54 Method B involves trying to estimate the
effect of the catchment area changes. It allows
us to include in the analysis not only trainees
from courts whose catchment area was constant but
also trainees from courts whose catchment area had
been changed, so long as we are able to estimate
and allow for the distorting effects consequent
upon that change. The way in which this works is
as follows. The major change in catchment area
was that a block of Manchester courts which had
been in Buckley Hall's catchment area was moved
into New Hall's catchment area. Trainees from
these courts do appear to have some quite
distinctive properties: they have more previous
convictions and a higher reconviction rate than
New Hall, Buckley Hall or Werrington House
trainees who came from courts whose catchment
areas were unchanged and are much more homogeneous
in these respects. This suggests that catchment
areas may be roughly equated, and hence bias due
to change in catchment area reduced, if we simply
estimate and control general differences between
trainees drawn from the Manchester courts
concerned and the remaining trainees. Method B is
thus able to analyse data on trainees from courts
whose catchment area was constant during the study

and trainees from courts whose catchment area shifted from Buckley Hall to New Hall. This amounts to about two thirds of the sample.

2.55 Method C uses the same method of estimating the distinctive effects associated with the block of courts which were moved from Buckley Hall's to New Hall's catchment area. Unlike method B however method C includes all cases for which we have data. The additional trainees will all have come from courts which changed catchment area. The form these catchment area changes took was however quite varied: it includes all the logically possible combinations of the three senior detention centres in the study together with cases drawn from courts which during either period I or period II were in the catchment area of a centre outside the study. Only a small number of cases was associated with each possible combination. We are unable to estimate the effects due to these catchment area changes and under method C we simply assume that they tend to cancel each other out and thus not greatly affect the results.

2.56 Our preferred technique for reducing bias due to catchment area changes is method B. In most cases we have however also analysed the data using one of the other methods and we discuss discrepancies between the results obtained from the different methods.

3.   REGIMES

INTRODUCTION

3.1   In setting out to evaluate the new regime in
detention centres, it was considered essential to
obtain, at first hand, qualitative descriptions of
the routines. It was hoped that such descriptions
would assist us in interpreting and discussing
more fully the results of the surveys involved in
the present study, and in addition that they would
prove particularly useful to those unfamiliar with
the daily running of detention centres.

3.2   Although research projects were carried out
in the early detention centres and there are
partial descriptions to be obtained, no blueprint
of the original regime exists. Descriptions in
this chapter provide a record of the operation of
the new regime. If for any purpose there is a
future need to know exactly what the Send and New
Hall regimes were like during the period of
evaluation, these close descriptions should meet
it.

3.3   Finally, whatever statement of the policy may
promise, it is the local staff who are ultimately
responsible for putting policy into effect.
Introducing changes in programme activity may be
an essential first step in changing the nature of
a regime but the way in which staff supervise new
activities will be a major determinant of the
trainees' experience. Local management can lead,
guide and correct staff, but proper implementation
of a defined regime depends on positive steps from
the staff themselves. The conversion of policy
into practical reality, therefore, involves a
chain of command in which the policy intentions,
as laid down in the Note of Guidance to Staff (see
Appendix A), may be variously interpreted at each

stage. It was felt that only by having an observer involved in each institution would it be possible to describe how policy had been put into practice.

3.4 Consequently, experienced observers were attached part-time to each of the pilot centres in order to monitor the process of change and the operation of the regimes. Each centre was visited over a considerable period of time (four months prior to the introduction of the new regime in April 1980 until well into 1981, with further visits in 1982) by a psychologist whose brief was to observe all of the routines in practice: receptions and discharges, early morning and late evening, night watch, adjudications, drill, parades, inspections, work periods, education and physical education. The main part of this chapter is the observers' report.

3.5 After the Home Secretary's announcement of the tougher regimes pilot project in October 1979, and prior to its implementation in April 1980, an intensive planning process took place resulting in the Note of Guidance to Staff (see Appendix A). This note, individual copies of which were made available to all members of staff two weeks before the start of the new regime, draws together in a single document the results of the previous six months planning in which the wardens of the centres were participants. It is the definitive statement of that regime and was the directive to staff on how they were to proceed. As well as outlining the overall aim of the project, the document defines what was to occur, describes the behaviour expected from staff as well as setting limits on that behaviour, and notes the constraints upon regime change (by statute and various practicalities). The Note of Guidance is thus the natural starting point for any observer of the changes that were introduced at Send and New Hall.

3.6 The Note's significance can best be
appreciated in the light of previous attempts to
create a fitting regime for detention centres.
This chapter begins, therefore, by briefly
considering the history of detention centres and
its impact on the present initiative. This is
followed by an analysis of the relationship
between the aims stated in the Note of Guidance
and the activities specified to achieve them
together with a short discussion of the problems
that the language in which the overall aims are
described presented to the evaluators. The main
part of the chapter then summarises the changes
that occurred when the pilot project was
introduced, outlines a number of the institutional
routines, and reaches tentative conclusions on the
implementation of the new regime.

3.7 The task of creating and running the first
detention centre regimes was allocated to the
Prison Commissioners although they had virtually
no experience of offenders aged under 17. Until
that time responsibility for those in that age
band had rested with the Home Office Children's
Department. Provisions were made from the start
to preserve that department's interest in and
access to the regimes in detention centres.

3.8 The Prison Commissioners, from the beginning,
stressed the separateness of detention centres
from prisons. Initially they wanted purpose-built
buildings although, in those times of economic
stringency, they were prepared to accept a
converted building in order to open the first
centre by 1952. It was not until much later, by
which time the principle of separateness had
become well established, that converted prison
buildings were used. The concept of separateness
was to be carried beyond accommodation; the new
centres were to be separated 'from the idea and
ambience of a prison' (Fox, 1952). In particular,

it was intended that staff would not wear uniforms and that the names of their various grades would be different from those in prisons.

3.9 In designing the regime itself, the Prison Commissioners had a considerable problem to resolve: if the task was to provide a deterrent, then the regime had to provide a jolt and if deterrence had to persist then so did the unpleasantness of that jolt. Clearly there were individual differences among the youths concerned, such that one might adjust with minimal upset to what another would find highly unpleasant and punitive. There was little room in the conception of detention centres for tailoring the degree of deterrence to individual differences; in fact, the planners were aware that a common high standard had to be an important feature of the regime. One which all would find continuously punitive was recognised as both impossible and abhorrent. The need to strike a balance between deterrent and constructive elements is apparent both in the Prison Commissioners' initial thinking and subsequently (Fox, 1952; Report of Commissioners of Prisons, 1952 et seq).

3.10 The statements of the first detention centre wardens about the regimes which they were endeavouring to implement (Elvy, 1952; Waylen, 1962) reveal a preoccupation with the integration of a deterrent regime with positive and reformative influences. They claim that all but a few inmates come to make physical, mental and moral progress. They deny that inmates are frightened into doing well; that they torture, torment or make life hell for them. The inmates are not cowed and they are not unhappy. Rather these works claim that deterrence is achieved by the deprivation of liberty, the provision of minimum physical amenities and a demand that

inmates lead a brisk and disciplined life
conforming to high standards in the areas of
politeness, self control, work and cleanliness.

3.11 Turning to the way individual inmates have
felt the impact of detention centres, there is
very little documented evidence and this is
perhaps understandable. Descriptive accounts
provided by inmates are mentioned in a number of
documents. These range from attestations of fair
treatment and good relationships with the staff
(Report of Commissioners of Prisons, 1953) to
complaints about being knocked about and fear of
circuit training (Dunlop and McCabe, 1965).
Allegations of rough treatment have led to
enquiries, both internal and otherwise (eg, Report
of the Work of the Prison Department, 1967,
paragraph 7; and Detention Centres: a report by
Sub Committee of the Friends Penal Affairs
Committee, 1968). Within the broad context of the
regimes in operation, there has obviously been
variation in the methods used to achieve what the
regime required.

3.12 Most commentators would agree that, over the
years, changes in the Prison Service and outside
in society have led to an increased emphasis being
placed on reformative elements in detention
centres. Six of the main changes are described
below:-

i.   Although a provision for formal education
       was included right at the start, it was
       expected that only a small proportion, those
       under the then school leaving age of 15,
       would have to be catered for. As the numbers
       of those receiving detention sentence under
       school age increased and as in 1972 the
       school leaving age was raised to 16, so it
       became necessary in junior detention centres
       to provide education for a large proportion

of the population, thereby affecting the style of the regime.

ii. Physical education was intended to be a major part of the detention centre regimes. In the early days physical training instructors tended to be particularly identified with strenuous aspects of the regime such as punishment exercises. Since then there has developed a service-wide philosophy of physical education that is generally independent of particular regimes, in which physical education is not to be associated with punishment since such punishment would be impossible to administer fairly, would detract from the real purpose of physical education and would put staff in an impossible position if an accident occurred.

iii. The reduction in the average working week (without overtime) in society generally has been reflected in the life of institutions - inmates work a shorter working week. The full time staff begin work later in the day and thus some of the impact of the early morning start has been reduced.

iv. The Criminal Justice Act 1961 brought about a number of changes which had an impact on the regimes in detention centres: the requirement that most sentences should be between three and six months was one factor which led to a move to introduce more of a 'training' ethos into the regime, especially for those serving a longer period. Compulsory after-care and the introduction of social workers enhanced the 'softening' in approach. It was originally intended that these new social workers should be women for 'experience has shown that the influence of women is a very useful adjunct to training', (Home Office

Circular 247/1968). On 1 January 1969,
responsibility for social work in detention
centres was taken over by the Probation and
After-Care Service.

v.   The seal on this progressive mellowing of the
     regime was the report of a conference held at
     Wakefield in 1966 of staff of all grades
     working in detention centres. It drew
     attention to the emphasis by this time not
     only on proper discipline and fast tempo but
     also on the establishment of relationships
     between individual members of staff and boys,
     and to the training and treatment aspects of
     detention (Report on the Work of the Prison
     Department, 1966, pages 22-23). This fitted
     with the concern expressed in the 11th Report
     from the House of Commons Estimates Committee
     (Prisons, Borstals and Detention Centres:
     Session 1966-7) that the centres were
     receiving boys with whom they were not
     intended to cope.

vi. Finally, the Report of the Advisory Council
     on the Penal System 'Detention Centres'
     (1970) suggested that:

          the punitive function of detention in a
          detention centre should be regarded as
          fulfilled by deprivation of the
          offender's liberty, and that treatment
          within the centre should be aimed at
          bringing about a change in the
          offender's behaviour. This requires
          that all aspects of the regime should be
          as constructive as possible and that
          there should be a greater emphasis on
          the individual. The majority of our
          detailed recommendations are concerned
          with the regime and are aimed at making
          treatment more effective and more

consistent with the philosophy above.
In particular, we consider that
increased emphasis should be placed on
education, both remedial and general
......

3.13 The tougher regimes pilot project may be seen
as an attempt to reinforce the deterrent element
in a system which had evolved considerably in a
reformative direction. However, the Note of
Guidance (the policy document outlining the form
of the new regime reproduced at Appendix A,)
reflects a concern to ensure that the new regime
should not become a brutal one. Thus, as well as
emphasising the more rigorous aspect of the new
regime 'hard constructive activities, discipline,
tidiness, drill parades and inspections',
(paragraphs 7-18), the document carefully
underlines more humane considerations ('staff will
be firm but fair' .... 'a focal point of the
project will be the interest taken by staff in the
progress and well being of the trainees') and
places important limitations on the behaviour of
the officers (....'just as it is important to
avoid standards slipping over time, so too it is
important that standards are not escalated or
distorted by unprofessional or unauthorised staff
practice.......').

3.14 Land (1975) raises the intriguing notion
that:-

    the original controversial detention centre
    project gained acceptance by being labelled
    experimental, because it is very difficult to
    oppose an experiment. Such a tactic allowed
    its proponents to remain vague about the
    actual methods to be employed in implementing
    the policy on the ground that it would
    restrict the experiment too much.

Whilst this criticism cannot be levelled at the
present initiative in that the regime changes are
specified in the Note of Guidance (paragraphs 7-
18), the relationship between those changes and
the overall aim is not unambiguous.

3.15 The overall aim of the project is to assess
whether young offenders can be effectively
deterred from committing further offences by
spending a period of weeks in a detention centre
with a more rigorous and demanding regime (Note of
Guidance, paragraph 1). There are really two
distinct problems posed by the aim so the
evaluation had to consider not only whether or not
young offenders were effectively deterred but also
whether the regime produced by seeking to
implement the Note of Guidance constituted one
which was more rigorous and demanding.

3.16 The Note of Guidance refers to a number of
things that are intended to produce a more
rigorous and demanding regime and these may be
usefully conceived as a hierarchy in which three
levels may be distinguished.

i.   In an attempt to deter, the trainees are to
      experience a regime that is both more
      rigorous and more demanding in nature.
      Rigour and demandingness are not objective
      features of a regime but are properties of
      the regime in relation to the characteristics
      of the individual (eg a demanding maths
      problem is a function of how good you are at
      mathematics - in other words, what each
      individual will find demanding will depend on
      his abilities and characteristics).

ii.   In order to achieve such a regime, the Note
      outlines a set of strategies, eg making the
      regime brisker, placing greater emphasis on

hard and constructive activities. These
statements of strategy indicate the kind of
change which it is expected will make a
regime rigorous and demanding but they do not
specify exactly what must be done.

iii. Finally there are actual tactics to be
employed and these make concrete the
strategies outlined above. Thus drill or the
introduction of more inspections are examples
of the actual tactics to be employed in order
to make the regime more brisk.

3.17 The relationship between the different levels
in the hierarchy is partly a matter of definition,
lower levels in the hierarchy being concrete
exemplifications of what is more abstractly
specified at a higher level in the hierarchy. For
instance, drill could be taken to be an example of
a brisk activity. So one might argue that the
introduction of drill necessarily, by definition,
means that the regime has become brisker.
Interpreting the hierarchy in this way is
attractive because it greatly simplifies the
evaluator's task. The bottom level of the
hierarchy is relatively simple to observe and
following this line one would assume that the
regime had (by definition) become more rigorous
and demanding if the specified tactics (drill, PE
etc) had been introduced. But the relationship
between the different levels in the hierarchy is
not simply one of definition. Drill may be by
definition a 'brisk activity' but whether it makes
the regime brisker than it was will depend upon
such things as how it is carried out (poorly
carried out drill can be a decidedly sloppy
affair), the nature of the activity that it
replaces (other activities can be briskly
conducted) and its more general impact on the
institution's routine (if the introduction of
drill broke up the time-table it might reduce the

64

briskness with which other, non-drill, activities were carried out, or alternatively it might increase the variety and pace of the daily routine).

3.18 The evaluation has had to take account of the complexity of this relationship, to note the concrete tactics introduced, but also separately to assess whether the regime has become brisker and has involved a greater emphasis on hard and constructive activities (the strategies), and whether the overall effect has been to produce a regime which is experienced by inmates as more rigorous and demanding.

3.19 This necessity created various methodological difficulties for us. The higher levels in the hierarchy are more difficult to assess in an uncontentious way. This is partly because they are specified more abstractly and hence are more difficult to interpret in terms of concrete observables. But it is also partly because the higher levels of the hierarchy refer not simply to objective features of the regime, but rather to the way in which trainees experience that regime. That is, whether a trainee finds a regime demanding depends not only on what demands are actually placed upon him but also upon how easily he is able to meet those demands.

METHOD

3.20 The observers began to visit the pilot centres at the beginning of 1980 and continued until late 1981 with further visits in 1982. In all, they spent about a quarter of their working time in the institutions during that period. In addition the control establishments for each of the pilot centres were visited. These visits were not, of course, as extensive but each observer spent up to two full weeks in the respective establishments.

3.21 The task given to the observers was to become known to and accepted by the staff; to be able to describe the range of elements central to the detention centre regime; to provide a full description of the daily routines throughout the sentence for the average trainee; and also to outline variations on this 'average' treatment.

3.22 In order to do this the observers attended the centres not only during the day but in the evening, at night, early in the morning, on weekends and on public holidays. These visits were made not once but many times in order to see the variations in routine brought about by such things as changes in staff, seasonal variation and fluctuations in the number of trainees in the institution.

3.23 Initially each observer met every member of staff in the pilot centres to explain the task in detail. The staff were assured of complete anonymity in order that they would not feel inhibited either about expressing their views or by the presence of the observer as they went about their daily work. Of course, the presence of an observer alters the situation for the participants and initially the staff were very wary about having the detail of their work overviewed. However, over the months that followed the staff became used to having an observer in the institution. Perhaps a good illustration of this acceptance is that the psychologist who visited Send continued to visit and was accepted by the staff during the industrial action which took place there early in 1980.

3.24 No part of the regime was closed to the observers, who were given their own set of keys and who had entry to the institutions at all hours of the day or night. Thus they were able to attend all staff meetings, the night-watch, the

reception and discharge as well as the more
ordinary parts of the working day. The Board of
Visitors also allowed them to attend their
meetings.

3.25 What follows is a condensed version of these
observations. It is intended that the
descriptions should provide a vivid picture of the
observers' view of the daily life in the pilot
centres.

3.26 For the reasons outlined above in the
discussion of the Note of Guidance it is difficult
to obtain unanimity about such things as the
'rigour' of the drill parade or of the 'hardness'
of the work the trainees performed and what is
presented in the following pages is the observers'
view or opinion of these activities. In that
sense the descriptions that follow are personal
views rather than objective data. However, these
descriptions are not intended to be the final word
on the implementation of the new regimes at Send
and New Hall. Rather they are intended to be an
additional source of information about what
happened in the pilot centres following the regime
changes, to be read in conjunction with the
information obtained from the staff and trainee
surveys. In the interest of style two conventions
have been adopted which require explanation.
First, except where changes had occurred during
the period of observation, the descriptive present
tense has generally been used in the accounts of
institutional routines. These of course relate to
the period of observation and it should not be
assumed that nothing has changed since then.
(Certain important subsequent changes are
mentioned in the chapter.) Secondly, the
descriptions are written in the third person and
avoid repetition of phrases such as 'in the
observers' view'. The chapter should, however, be
read as the account of the psychologist observers

who, while having no particular stance vis-a-vis
the new regimes, are presenting an essentially
personal account.

THE INSTITUTIONS AND THEIR ROUTINES

3.27 The aim of this section is to present a close
description of the life in the two detention
centres, to note changes in practice as a result
of the present initiative, and to provide a record
of the regimes at New Hall and Send.

**Setting the scene: description of New Hall and
Send**

a.   **New Hall**

3.28 New Hall detention centre's main buildings
lie among the trees in attractive upland country
midway between Wakefield and Huddersfield. It is
a fairly remote spot, particularly in the winter-
time when approach roads soon become blocked with
snow[1], and although the nearby small towns have
grown up around industry and mining, the
surrounding district is decidedly rural. Visiting
by public transport is both difficult and time
consuming.

3.29 The establishment was opened in 1936 as an
open prison farm camp for selected prisoners from
Wakefield. It was assembled rather than purpose
built. The wooden huts of which the camp was
composed had previously been used to house
conscripts during the First World War. Since that
time the row of huts which comprise most of the

---

[1] The psychologist attached to Send detention centre was
particularly struck by this aspect when on a visit to New
Hall he came upon an abandoned police car in a snowdrift!

sleeping accommodation, together with the old
gymnasium brought back into use for the new
regime, have been linked by a long straight
corridor leading into the administration block
beyond.

3.30 The original huts have been augmented in
recent years by modern single storied buildings
and some of the original dormitories have reached
the limits of their life, one having been
demolished and another heavily buttressed.
Nevertheless, the layout is functional and is well
suited to its purpose. A modern kitchen and
dining hall, chapel, hospital, and education
blocks have been built onto the long corridor.
Movement about the centre is straightforward,
supervision is much easier and more effective than
in many detention centres, and the overall
appearance is clean and bright and by prison
service standards, airy.

3.31 During the early years, Wakefield prisoners
cleared over 70 acres of woodland to form the
present Wakegate farm (the detention centre's
farm) and the area now enclosed within the
perimeter fence. Some woodland remains but most
of the estate is given over to grazing (now
130 acres). The farm buildings cater for a herd
of 80 dairy cows and, in addition to pens and
areas for storing fodder, contain a milking
parlour and refrigeration plant. The nearby
piggery houses a large number of breeding sows.
Under the supervision of farm staff and discipline
officers, trainees carry out the milking, are
responsible for feeding the animals and carry out
much of the manual work on the farm.

3.32 About two and a half acres of land enclosed
within the perimeter wire is given over to market
gardening. Vegetable and salad crops are grown

for consumption in the centre and, in recent years, greater use has been made of plastic growing tunnels. A greenhouse, an office and a store holding garden equipment are also located there. Poor drainage means that much of the ground used to be water-logged during the wetter, cooler months. This remains a problem although some improvements have been made.

3.33 On the other side of the detention centre but also within the perimeter fence is a sportsfield. Here, too, heavy soil drains slowly and for some periods of the year the two football pitches are not usable.

3.34 In addition to those buildings already mentioned as adjoining the main corridor, a large and modern gymnasium, together with an outdoor basketball pitch, lie to one side; stores, a loomshop, works department, boiler house, the Catholic chapel and the parade ground to the other. Great pride is taken in the gardens and grassed areas which surround these buildings and on a sunny summer's day the detention centre presents a tidy and very attractive appearance. In winter by contrast it can be a most inhospitable place. The higher than average rainfall, frequent and heavy snow falls and its position high up and exposed to the wind make the lot of the trainees in winter much more unpleasant than in summer.

3.35 The quarters in which some of the staff live lie within the same wooded area. Set some distance from any public roads, and with the nearest villages a mile or so away, New Hall is a very compact and self-contained community. But its physical isolation is not reflected in any great social isolation. Many of the civilian and uniformed staff are native to the area and several officers worked locally as tradesmen or miners before joining the Prison Service. The evening class teachers provide further close links with the community.

3.36 So, despite the physical separation of New Hall, its staff are very much members of the local community. In the past these links were given greater currency by work in the community undertaken by a few trainees, for example, looking after a local churchyard or clearing snow and ice from old people's paths in winter. However, following the introduction of the new regime with its tightly programmed activities, only one such community service project has been retained, in which two trainees nearing discharge assist at weekends in a nearby home for the physically handicapped. During the year of the disabled (1981), trainees helped to raise money for disabled young people in the neighbouring village.

3.37 On a typical day during the period of observation New Hall would be holding about 100 trainees although the population could vary considerably within a short space of time from a low of about 70, at which point it became difficult to maintain essential services, to a ceiling of about 125 when accommodation would be packed tight and the sewage system barely able to cope. Most trainees are housed in four secure dormitories, though all will have spent their first few nights at the centre in small individual rooms known as cubicles. Since New Hall is a senior detention centre, the trainees are aged 17-20 years on reception.

b. **Send**

3.38 Send detention centre is, in fact, nearer the villages of East Clandon and Ripley and some distance away from the town of Send. It is in the Surrey commuter belt about 25 miles from central

London. Whilst the warden[2] makes great effort to integrate the centre into the life of the countryside (from gym displays at the local fetes to the steaming Xmas pudding for a community of nuns), there is a sense in which the detention centre is not part of the community in which it is placed.

3.39 The centre was purpose built in the 1960s on the site of an isolation hospital. The architecture is domestic - a series of interconnecting one storied buildings set among grass and flower beds. There are many windows so the dormitories are light and airy and easily supervised. The prospect on entering the gates resembles an English suburban garden.

3.40 There is a reception area, three main dormitories and the induction unit with individual cubicles, dining room, kitchen, laundry, chapel, two gymnasiums (one added for the new regime, converted from the former cassette workshop), school, visits room, large playing field, small parade ground, market gardens and the administration block. The establishment is bounded by a 17 foot high chain-mesh fence. Outside the fence there are some officers' quarters, a club for the staff and a playing area known as 'The Green' for the children of the staff.

3.41 The accommodation is bright, pleasant and resembles a school more than a prison. It is not lavish, however, and up to 1980 was liable to be cramped following the heavy seasonal influxes from the courts.

---

[2] Since 24 May 1983 the term 'warden' has been replaced by 'governor'.

3.42 Send is a junior detention centre, accommodating up to 118 trainees, aged between 14 and 16 years. Since many of the trainees are therefore below school leaving age, education is a major part of the daytime routine. At New Hall it is largely an evening activity.

The period before the introduction of the new regime

3.43 Both New Hall and Send were opened as senior detention centres in the early sixties and a few of the staff who worked in them during those early years work there still. The regime operating even in the early sixties had moved away from the concept of the 'short, sharp, shock' of the very first detention centres but the emphasis was still on discipline and obedience, cleanliness, tidiness and a very brisk routine. In the following years a number of changes took place, some as a matter of official policy, some reflecting the broader changes in the prison service as a whole, and others resulting from the differing concerns of successive wardens. These changes affected content as well as style and emphasis. Send, which had been a senior detention centre, was redesignated a junior one and, as a result, daytime education became a much more significant part of the daily activity. Drill ceased to be practised in either centre and work parties walked in formation rather than marched to and from work. Social workers (later probation officers) were introduced in an attempt to cater for the individual needs of trainees. But in 1979, when the new initiative was announced, the pace was still brisk, standards of cleanliness and tidiness were high (for example, there was an almost total absence of graffiti of any kind in the institution buildings), thorough inspections still played an important part in maintaining these standards, and staff saw it as central to their task to maintain the pace of the regime and to ensure that trainees

did not 'cut any corners'. Nevertheless,
particularly at New Hall, the atmosphere was
friendly if not really relaxed and the more
leisured periods of the day were characterised by
the cheerful banter among and between trainees and
uniformed staff. Standards required of the
trainees were probably not so very different from
what they had always been but physical demands
were almost certainly less and relations between
trainees and most staff had warmed considerably.

3.44 When the Home Secretary announced on 10
October 1979 that New Hall and Send were the two
detention centres chosen to operate the pilot
project, the immediate response of most staff in
both institutions was one of a certain pride at
having been selected but also of some
apprehension. The initiative appeared 'right' to
many of the staff in that it fitted their personal
views (especially at Send) on how criminal
behaviour should be dealt with. However,
particularly at New Hall, there was some
apprehension since some had memories of those
earlier years when the regime had been more
unyielding and less responsive to individual
limitations. They recalled the times when
allegations had been made against staff, and
inquiries held, and they were concerned lest the
regime, in demanding more of the trainees, would
demand much more of the officers. In particular
they recognised that the narrow area between
failing to maintain adequate control on the one
hand and overstepping the limits of their
discipline code on the other would be made
narrower still.

3.45 The months after the Home Secretary's
announcement were an incubation period for the
fears and suspicions of staff and these were
aggravated by the media interest at the time. At
New Hall some staff were concerned at the prospect

of the re-introduction of drill, at the reduction
in time spent by trainees on work which would
result from the inclusion of drill and extra PE in
the programme, and at the likely closure of the
construction industries course. At Send most
discipline staff welcomed the re-introduction of
drill and the change into uniform but were worried
that the extra activities would over-programme an
already full day. The education staff regretted
the loss of education time and, with the physical
education staff, what they saw as a reduction in
the variety and scope of their respective
programmes. Although a series of local meetings
were held, many staff were left with the feeling
that the new regimes were based on insufficient
practical knowledge of detention centres and that
their own views had not been adequately taken into
account. In March 1980 short training courses in
drilling methods helped improve staff morale.
Uncertainties returned as the date for introducing
drill approached, but there seemed at this stage
to be a greater preparedness amongst the staff to
cope with the demands of the new regime.

Changes in regime in Send and New Hall

3.46 The following is a summary of the main
changes that resulted from the implementation of
the regime.

a. **Send**

  i.   Send ceased to receive trainees
        sentenced to more than three months
        detention centre training. Previously
        it had received a very small number of
        trainees with six months' sentences.

  ii.   Staff at Send were to dress in prison
        uniform. Hitherto staff in junior

detention centres wore civilian clothes.

iii. Formal drill sessions were introduced. Before the implementation of the new regime, parades and inspections and a form of movement in which trainees were required to 'walk smartly' from one activity to another already took place at Send but formal drill sessions were an addition. The number of parades and inspections was increased.

iv. Physical education was increased from 1 hour to an average of 1 hour 20 minutes per day - in practice seven rather than five one-hour sessions per week. Increased emphasis was placed on such activities as circuit training, weight training, gymnastics and running at the expense of physical skills teaching.

v. Because most physical education was timetabled during the daytime, the time available for daytime education was reduced by one-third. Enamelling, pottery, soft toy-making and stone polishing were considered inappropriate for the tougher regime and were replaced by woodwork and, later, metalwork.

vi. The workshop where trainees broke up faulty cassettes was converted to an extra gymnasium at minimum cost, and market gardening work was increased. The strengths and supervision of other work parties were adjusted.

vii. All trainees considered by the medical officer to be physically or mentally unfit for the new regime were to be transferred to a centre not operating it. Previously, any trainee who had a disability usually followed a regime tailored to his needs.

viii. The certified maximum accommodation was reduced from 130 to 126 in recognition that overcrowding would hinder the operation of the new regime. This followed industrial action by discipline staff two months earlier which lasted for five days until the roll (which had risen to 126) fell.

ix. A four day induction period was formalised for new receptions. During this period they were available for the induction tests and interviews but more importantly were kept together in order to learn how to drill and keep their kit in the required manner without disrupting the routine of the more experienced trainees.

x. Evening lights out was brought forward from 10.00 pm to 9.30 pm.

xi. As well as these changes in routine a number of staffing modifications were made. The staff complement was increased initially by five: a principal officer, a physical education instructor, two gardens officer instructors[3] and a hospital senior officer. In addition, two prison

---

[3] The complement of garden instructors soon afterwards was reduced from four to three.

officers were posted in to bring their numbers up to complement. All of these staff changes can be understood in terms of the increased requirement from the regime: the hospital officer because the medical supervision of trainees increased (particularly to select-out those who were unfit); the physical education officer and gardens officer because of the extra demand on those departments; the principal officer strengthened supervision in the establishment and a greater continuity in staff deployment became possible. After the introduction of the new regime, for example, officers were deployed to particular dormitories thereby providing greater supervision of the trainees at that point. This greater flexibility of staff also meant that the staff break periods could be used to drill and parade the boys rather than simply have them standing 'at ease' as was the case previously.

b.   **New Hall**

i.   New Hall ceased to receive trainees sentenced to more than three months. Previously about one-third of New Hall trainees had six months' sentences (for exact figures, see Table 7.1).

ii.   Formal drill sessions were introduced. Initially the trainees were drilled in two groups depending on work party: one directly after breakfast and the other after lunch[4]. The number of parades and inspections was increased.

---

[4]   After September 1980 all trainees drilled for one hour after lunch.

iii. The extra PE required by the Note of Guidance was organised by the addition of two extra PE sessions each week. Thus trainees on two days of each week would have PE both in the morning and in the afternoon and on three days would have it once a day as in the old timetable. Visits by selected trainees for swimming instruction at the public baths were stopped. The PE evening classes covering weightlifting, basketball, volleyball, football, gymnastics and multi-gym were retained. The content of the additional daytime PE was restricted to the non-recreational end of the PE programme. The old gymnasium at New Hall was refurbished and brought into operation, thus providing additional space to cater for the increased activities.

iv. As at Send all trainees considered by the medical officer to be physically or mentally unfit for the new regime were to be transferred (normally to Buckley Hall detention centre).

v. The construction industry course designed to develop the basic skills required of a building labourer and offering places for eight trainees was closed.

vi. The kitchen and maintenance work parties were reduced and the farming, cleaning and weaving shop parties were increased.

vii. Weekday evening association was reduced from 45 to 30 minutes.

viii. Evening lights out was brought forward from 10.00 pm to 9.30 pm.

ix. The certified maximum accommodation remained the same, unlike at Send where it was reduced.

x. As at Send the staff complement was strengthened slightly: an extra hospital officer to cope with increased medical checks; an extra principal officer and an extra PE instructor to cater for the extra PE. The number of discipline staff was brought up to strength: this enabled all four dormitories to be supervised at locking and unlocking periods. One civilian instructor post was relinquished when the skilled labourers course was terminated.

Arrival and reception

3.47 The new receptions arrive direct from court, either with a prison escort or more frequently in a police car. For many of them it is their first experience of a prison department establishment, although some may have spent time remanded in custody. For a few it is the first time they have been away from home. For most it is a traumatic experience. The staff believe that the first few days have the greatest impact, and it is this sense of shock from the trainee that underlies that impression. Few, if any, are truculent at this point.

3.48 The trainees enter the reception office often still handcuffed. They are expected to stand erect and smartly (though not to attention) whilst the reception officer asks his questions. The purpose of the reception procedure is to check and record information. It involves ensuring that the trainee is lawfully held, checking, recording and

storing his property and obtaining from him
essential details, such as address, date of birth,
next of kin and place of last custody. Having
previously been given a towel[5] to wrap himself in
when he has removed all his clothing, the trainee
undresses in front of two officers[6] and, as each
article of clothing is removed, it is placed in a
box and recorded and described on an official
form. This part of the process is very matter of
fact.

3.49 The trainee bathes, is issued with clean
detention centre clothing, is fed, seen by the
hospital officer (the following morning he will be
examined by the medical officer) and then housed
that night in a single room (cubicle). He will
remain there for several nights until he is moved
to dormitory accommodation. In the meantime he
will start doing PE, drill, work and education.

a.   **Send**

3.50 At Send the officers wear uniforms under the
new system. For trainees who have not been in
custody before, this may heighten the sense of
being in a penal establishment. The reception
procedure is very formal. When the police car
arrives both officers are waiting. The post of

---

[5]   Following an inspection by the Prison Department
Inspectorate prior to the setting up of the new regime,
provision was made at New Hall for dressing gowns and
slippers to be available for those trainees needing to be
taken to see the hospital officer, for example. More
recently a dressing gown and slippers have been made
available as a matter of routine at Send.

[6]   Two officers are required to be present to ensure that the
correct procedure is carried out meticulously and to
protect the staff against allegations of ill treatment.

reception officer is a fixed one, so it is the
same officers who carry out the reception process.
The boy is hurried from the car and into the
building, moving very fast. An officer stands
very close to him and shouts commands. The
officers behave like stereotype sergeant majors
because they are convinced of the value of setting
the tone of the place at the start. They believe
that a strict reception and induction procedure is
an essential control mechanism for an institution
that has a high turnover of trainees. There is
rarely personal animosity towards a particular
trainee. Instead officers tend to have a somewhat
jaundiced view of the whole class. This is
perhaps inevitable given that the stream of young
offenders passing through Send is unending. The
observer noticed cases where offenders who
appeared unconventional, such as punks, effeminate
trainees or those with rastafarian dreadlocks,
were treated in a manner tinged with contempt.
But procedures were tightened up during the period
of observation and the atmosphere during the
reception became more formal and professional.

b.   **New Hall**

3.51 The trainee is expected to behave smartly
while the officer asks his questions. It is made
clear at the outset that the trainee must address
the officer as 'sir' but there are few other
demands. The emphasis is on the swift recording
and checking of information. There are occasional
lighter moments too, as when a trainee's towel
slipped momentarily from his grasp: as he,
blushing, struggled to recover his modesty, the
officer looked up from his record keeping and in
his distinctive Yorkshire accent said 'Ee lad, art
tha' tryin' to frighten me?'. The trainee grinned
and survived the experience without too much loss
of dignity. This incident illustrates that during
the reception procedure there is no intention to

impress with strictness or impersonal discipline and no attempt to demean or insult the trainee. Standards of politeness and responsiveness are set and the reception officer makes careful note of the trainee's response.

3.52 The story of the trainee's towel perhaps illustrates the difference in the reception in Send and New Hall. Although it would be wrong to say that there are never light moments, the strictness is more conspicuous at Send than at New Hall.

Medical examinations

3.53 All trainees entering the centres are seen by the hospital officer on reception and again by the medical officer (a local general practitioner) the following morning without fail. Medical checks in all detention centres were thorough even before the introduction of the pilot project. Since then examinations in centres taking part in the pilot project have had to consider specifically whether the trainee is physically or mentally fit for the tougher regime.

3.54 On the evening of reception the hospital officer examines each new trainee recording his height, weight, and any apparent illnesses or infestations. He measures the trainee's blood pressure and peak respiratory flow, takes and tests a urine sample, checks vision and hearing, and interviews the trainee about his past medical history, any morbid family history, any involvement with drugs, any evidence of heavy drinking or an alcohol problem, previous suicide attempts or psychiatric history. At New Hall, in addition the trainee is offered a tetanus injection in readiness for work on the farm. All are told about the procedure for obtaining medical attention during sentence and are advised that they will be seen next day by the medical officer.

3.55 Next morning the medical officer carries out
a routine but thorough medical check. Further
questions are put about the trainee's health and
how he is feeling at the time. The trainee strips
to his underpants and the medical officer examines
him, checking his pulse, breathing, ears, mouth
and throat, hands and feet; he notes and questions
any scars or signs of injury. It is a thorough
examination in which the medical officer has due
regard for the physical demands that are to be
made of the trainees.

3.56 If the trainee is given a clean bill of
health he will remain at New Hall or Send. If he
is medically unfit for the tougher regime he will
be transferred to a detention centre that is not
part of the pilot project. A few trainees,
considered likely to be fully fit for the regime
within a matter of days, are retained. There is
no significant difference between Send and New
Hall in this medical routine.

The warden's interview

3.57 All the trainees who have been received the
previous evening are interviewed by the warden or
deputy warden next day. They are lined up outside
the office in which the interviews, grade reviews
and adjudications take place. The warden sits at
a desk in front of which there is a square known
as the 'mat'. The warden has in front of him the
files of the boys he is about to see, including
the medical officer's report, and those completed
by the reception officer. The warden's interview
is the same in each case. The boy bounds into the
office with that peculiar walk/run characteristic
of all inmates' movement about the institution.
It appears awkward and self-conscious from the new
trainees. The chief's clerk calls to him to stand
to attention on the mat and give name and number
to the warden. The numbers attached to the

trainees' names do not roll easily off their
tongues. Some smile bashfully, but in order to
make it clear that 'this is no holiday camp, but
one of Her Majesty's prisons'[7] any response that
falls short of standard has to be repeated. The
warden then tells the new trainee to 'stand at
ease, hands behind back, feet 15 inches apart,
relax without flopping'. Then information, such
as number, court, sentence, age, religion and
whether or not the boy expects his parents to
visit is checked against the record in front of
him. It is done swiftly, the bureaucracy softened
by such catch phrases as 'and you're Roman
Catholic in case I have to bury you?' At the
mention of parents visiting, it is not uncommon
for a boy to well up with tears. The message that
he has brought this on himself and grief to his
parents is rammed home but the atmosphere is
gruffly caring. The warden has in all probability
visited him in his cell the previous night when he
was writing letters home (a requirement for all
those who have contact with parents). The warden
then delivers the same homily to each one, telling
him that he expects 'effort and behaviour'. He
describes the system of points awarded each day
for these two virtues, a maximum of 50 achievable
in one week: 'but that's impossible, since only
the warden is perfect'. The property list is
checked off with the boy agreeing that this is
what was taken from him on reception. All
property is stored until release except that
opened packets of cigarettes are flushed down the
lavatory.

3.58 The warden's interview sets the tone for the
others. The purpose is to bring home the standard

---

[7] Send is often inadvertently referred to by staff as if it
were a prison.

of behaviour required from the trainees, and to
act as a formal check on the property and well-
being of the trainee.

3.59 The trainees are reminded that they are in a
detention centre and subject to its discipline.
The philosophy underlying the orderliness of
detention centre life is undoubtedly foreign to
most of the trainees. Most of them adapt quickly
to the constraints imposed upon them. The 'sir
(or madam)' ending to each sentence is quickly
learned, so that when the warden concludes his
interview with 'have you questions to ask me lad'
the reply 'no sir' comes more readily to their
lips. He then informs some of them 'yes, you have
lad: the way to the nearest hairdresser'. Such
homely jests are employed to reassure the
trainees, who have for the most part spent a
difficult night, whilst leaving them in no doubt
of what is expected. The brisk walk/run is
performed more easily on leaving the office.

3.60 At New Hall the form of the interview is
essentially the same, although of course there are
differences in personal style.

3.61 All trainees are seen by a probation officer
at least twice during their sentence (in a few
cases there is a great deal of contact). The
initial interview takes place on the first working
day after reception[8]. Matters covered include
where the boy has been living immediately prior to
sentence; is he in contact with his family; are

---

[8] Since May 1983 when Part I of the Criminal Justice Act
1982 was implemented, the role of the probation officer
has become generally a liaison one and there has been a
greater emphasis on the involvement of discipline staff in
the throughcare of the trainee.

there any immediate family or emotional problems
that might prey on his mind during his sentence;
where he will go on release; are the
social/probation services in touch with him etc.
(The warden's interview will have covered much of
this ground but the trainee may feel more able to
talk about any personal problems in the less
formal atmosphere of the probation office).

3.62 The probation officers in post at Send during
this period saw their task as being somewhat at
variance with that of the prison officer: their
job was to care for and help the offender with his
problems, not to discipline him. They felt the
one to one interview in a private office was
important for the boy who might have had a
traumatic night on reception and who might need
somewhere quiet to let out his fears and his
distress. Trainees could ask to see a probation
officer at any time during sentence. Requests
were generally of a practical nature or about
family matters. At New Hall, while the probation
staff's objectives and procedures for achieving
them were closely similar to those at Send, there
was far less of a division between the probation
officers and their prison officer colleagues.
There was a considerable flow of information
between the probation department and house staff
(officers). In practice the roles were seen as
complementary and co-operative rather than as
opposite or unrelated.

The grade system

3.63 Trainees are also interviewed by the warden
for grade promotion.

3.64 At Send there are three grades of trainee,
each distinguished by a differently coloured tie.
Trainees become eligible to be considered for

their grade promotion after three weeks. The
decision is based on house, work, PE and education
reports. Trainees learn about the grade system on
their first night from their induction leaflet,
because getting one's grade is intended to be seen
as an integral part of the whole experience. The
majority of boys are promoted to grade two on
their first appearance and at any one time
approximately one third to one half of the
trainees will be in grade two. Those promoted in
grade become eligible for selection to an outside
working party although some other considerations
such as certain offence types would preclude
selection for outside work. Selection to grade
three is much rarer and boys in this grade occupy
a separate dormitory.

3.65 At New Hall there are only two grades, again
distinguished by differently coloured ties;
eligibility for consideration for grade two here
occurs slightly earlier than at Send, between 15
and 19 days into sentence (depending on which day
of the week the sentence was given). The decision
is based on work, PE and house reports and it is
stressed that the grade will be given in relation
to behaviour, industry and effort. About four
fifths get their grade on the first occasion. As
this process occurs slightly earlier at New Hall
in a sentence which itself is usually two weeks
longer in a senior rather than a junior centre,
approximately two thirds are in grade two at any
one time. Again, with promotion trainees become
eligible for selection for work outside. Whilst
before the pilot project regime there were certain
advantages or privileges at New Hall associated
with getting one's grade and having seniority
(access to table tennis and darts during evening
association and transfer to a 'trustee'
dormitory), after the start of the new regime all
of the dormitories were equally supervised and
opportunities for the additional recreation

activities became rare and limited association time curtailed association activities for both grades. However, in both establishments getting one's grade was still prized by trainees.

Education tests

a. Send

3.66 On their second day at Send all trainees are brought to the education department to take the NFER Reading Test (NF6) and the Staffordshire maths test. Trainees who score low on the reading test are given a further examination using the Holborn Reading Scale. All of those who are below school leaving age are enrolled in compulsory daytime education classes. Those who are over 16 years may be enrolled in remedial classes according to their test results. Otherwise they will attend maintenance[9] or evening education classes.

b. New Hall

3.67 As all of the trainees are over school leaving age, education does not feature so prominently at New Hall. Nevertheless all trainees are tested as at Send and in addition complete an intelligence test. Those whose attainment is below 10.5 years in reading are offered remedial reading classes. The emphasis in these classes is not just on basic reading ability but on developing confidence and communication skills. Under the new regime there has been a marginal reduction in the numbers undergoing

---

[9] Maintenance education classes are provided for a few of those over 16 who were attending school education classes or courses before sentence.

remedial classes. In practice these are confined
to the 15 trainees in the population who need it
most.

Physical education tests

3.68 Before the implementation of the pilot
project, a medical report certified which areas of
physical education boys were fit to take part in.
Some boys were given light exercises to do, others
were excused contact sports for reasons such as
heart or chest problems, old fractures or previous
injuries. Since the introduction of the new
regime trainees found to be physically or mentally
unfit to take part in the regime as a whole have
been transferred to other establishments.

3.69 Trainees enter the gymnasium via the changing
room. They are given five minutes to change into
gym clothes and present themselves in the
gymnasium, standing to attention, their day
clothes folded edge to edge and stacked
unsupported in front of them. At first they have
difficulty in stacking the clothes correctly.
However, it is a skill they are expected to master
during the induction phase (there is kit folding
practice in the cubicles). These stacks are
inspected by the instructor and commented on. At
a command the boys run to place their kit on
shelves in the changing room and they return at
the double to line up once more in the gymnasium.
The first gym they experience is a test session.
They complete a series of exercises involving
timed runs, jumping, pull-ups and weight training
activities and their scores are recorded on
personal cards.

Overview of induction

3.70 The work trainees start on is cleaning the
centre. This is very thoroughly supervised and

includes a lot of elbow work. As indicated above
they undergo education tests and encounter their
first taste of the physical education which forms
such a major part of detention centre training.
They also learn how to drill (described below).
Any spare time is spent in their cubicles learning
to fold and care for their 'kit' ie clothes, bed
and boots. With the exception of items they are
allowed to buy in the canteen everything they have
is provided by the centre and is treated as
'government property'. The kit is laid out when
not in use in a highly regulated way. Toiletries
such as soap, shaving materials, tooth-powder and
comb are placed on top of the locker in precisely
the same order for each trainee. Boots, plimsolls
and slippers when not being worn are located in
the one order under the bed, pyjamas and vest are
folded edge to edge and in such a way that they
can be stacked unsupported on top of the locker
(at Send) or in the locker (at New Hall) (see
Figure 3.1). The bed is always perfectly made in
a hospital or military manner. At New Hall each
morning, the blankets, sheets and bed-rug have to
be stripped from the bed and folded and stacked in
regulation fashion.

[10] The diagram represents the kit layout required at New Hall. It is similar in most respects to the one at Send.

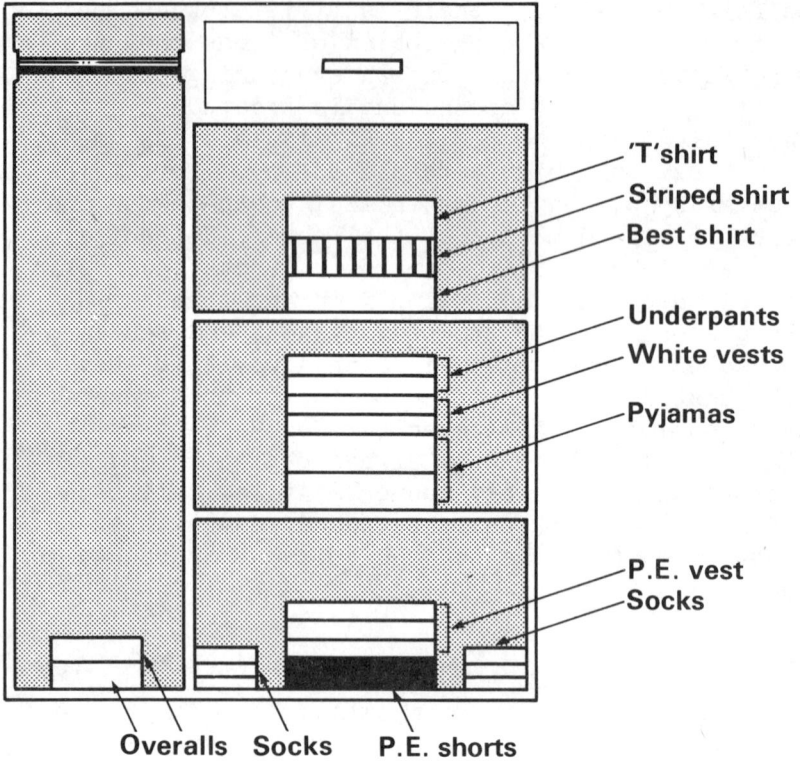

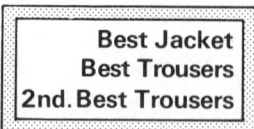

'T'shirt
Striped shirt
Best shirt

Underpants
White vests
Pyjamas

P.E. vest
Socks

Overalls   Socks   P.E. shorts

Best Jacket Best Trousers 2nd. Best Trousers	DURING THE DAY Folded neatly on hangers over the bottom of the bed AT NIGHT Hung up in the locker
Towels	Folded over the bed head with blue coloured edge to the end
Pullovers	When issued, folded on top of Overalls

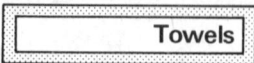

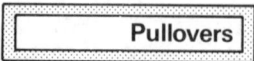

Figure 3.1

3.71 At Send trainees are transferred into the
dormitories after four days in the induction unit.
At New Hall trainees are transferred out of the
cubicles to the dormitories after a few days,
depending on the space available in the
dormitories and the trainee's readiness for
dormitory living.

Overview of a day

a.   **Send**

3.72 The population is divided into 10 groups in
order to facilitate distribution to the various
drill, work, PE and education activities. In the
pre-breakfast period the boys wash, dress, clean
the dormitory ready for inspection and make
applications (to see the warden, the medical
officer, the probation officer etc). At 8.00 am
there is assembly on the parade ground. After
that trainees go to drill, PE, work and (from 9.00
am) education by groups. The afternoon activities
are similar to those in the morning except that
the groups change about. There is another parade
and those who have been to school in the morning
work in the afternoon. After tea, the trainees
spend the half hour before evening classes
cleaning their boots, shoes and dormitory. After
supper at 8.30 pm the trainees wash, change
underwear and socks, dress in pyjamas and go to
bed. There they read or converse across the
dormitory, rather as in a hospital (provided, of
course, that noise level is kept low) until lock
up. The regime at weekends is of course
different: there is no classroom education, and in
work there is an emphasis on cleaning tasks. On
Saturday there is the warden's inspection on the
drill square which is something special, like a
ceremonial parade. On Sunday the warden inspects
the living quarters. On both afternoons sport is
organised and in the evening all trainees are

allowed to watch television for two hours. Visits
from families can take place every day but occur
mainly at weekends[11] , and there is opportunity for
the boys to write letters home.

b. **New Hall**

3.73 The pattern of the day is similar but there
are some important differences. Since there are
no schoolboys at New Hall only those boys in
remedial education have daytime classes and then
only in the morning. A very small number of
trainees for whom it is judged essential to
continue vocational courses, which were
interrupted by the detention centre sentence, are
allowed to continue on maintenance classes. This
involves up to two hours a day in the education
department plus relevant study in the evenings and
perhaps a kind of day release back to their
college if it is near enough in the second four
weeks of their sentence.

3.74 Thus senior trainees spend both morning and
afternoon at work and as a result their day is
less varied. The two extra PE sessions per week
take place for most trainees during the daytime
rather than in the evening as at Send. In
addition since September 1980 the drill session
has been done by the whole population at the same
time after lunch and not group by group as at
Send. These apparently minor differences mean
that there is less movement about the institution
at New Hall and less variety in the trainees' day.

---

[11] Since the introduction of the project visits have been
possible on Sundays and Bank holidays.

94

Unlocking

a.   New Hall

3.75 The day begins for the majority of the
trainees at about 6.15 am. For those who make up
the stock party it begins 45 minutes earlier and
by 6.15 am they will have been working for a
quarter of an hour. The immediate task for those
who remain is to get out of night clothes into
jeans and slippers, to strip their beds and make
up bedpacks, and to begin thoroughly to clean and
tidy the dormitory and accompanying toilet area.

3.76 This process is interrupted by the arrival of
the daytime staff at 6.45 am. Trainees have to
stand by their beds in silence while the roll is
checked. All of the dormitories are at this point
under more or less constant supervision by an
officer and the pace of working at cleaning the
dormitories quickens. By and large the officers
do not organise the work. It is up to the
trainees themselves to achieve the required
standard although some officers do offer a little
advice as the time for inspection approaches.
During this period all trainees have to wash and
shave. Time is short and so about 100 trainees
have to pass through in about 20 minutes. The
tempo is brisk and staff have to hurry those
trainees who appear to be wasting time. Quietness
and restraint are demanded but there is no rule of
complete silence at this point.

3.77 After washing, trainees complete their work
in the dormitory, put on second best uniform and
arrange their kit neatly in their lockers ready
for inspection. The inspection is carried out by
the senior officer present.

3.78 Standards for the appearance of the dormitory
can be fairly closely defined and include the

following. The floor has to be clean, dust-free,
and free from rubber or shoe polish marks. This
applies even under the beds and the lockers. All
surfaces (locker tops, window ledges and the tops
of the windows, heating pipes and the frameworks
of the beds) have to be clean and dust free. Beds
have to be in line, each covered by the bed rug,
with bedpacks located at the head of the bed.
Lockers have to be in line, drawers and doors
open, insides clean and dust-free. Bedpacks have
to be 'square' with sheets and blankets folded to
the correct width and arranged in the set order.
No edges should show. Pillows are to lie against
the head of the bed at an angle of 45°. Clothing
kit is to be set out in the lockers in the
prescribed order with individual items of clothing
'boxed' so as to present flat sides and sharp
edges. Footwear has to be clean and polished and
lined up under the bed. Small towels have to be
folded neatly over the locker towel rails and
larger towels have to be folded over the locker
doors. Toilets and washbasins have to be clean
and dry. Trainees must stand to attention
throughout and be silent except when invited to
speak.

3.79 The purpose of the inspection is to maintain
good trainee and institution standards. It is not
carried out in a way designed to increase stress
or to demoralise the trainees. In the course of
the inspection individual faults are pointed out
and are expected to be rectified.

3.80 Once inspection of the dormitory has been
satisfactorily completed any trainees reporting
sick or requiring treatment are sent to the
hospital. The other trainees proceed in single
file to the breakfast queue. They are supposed
not to talk or move out of line but so long as
trainees' behaviour remains moderate supervision

is not greatly in evidence. Breakfast is a
relatively relaxed period, as are all meals. Each
trainee has his own place and has to sit there for
every meal. Those from the same dormitory do not
necessarily sit together. Talking is permitted at
meals provided it does not become too loud and the
meal is a social occasion rather than just food.
However cleanliness and good manners are insisted
upon. Acceptable behaviour in the dining hall is
maintained without the need for close supervision.

b.   **Send**

3.81 This period is very similar. The kit layout
requirement is just as rigorous. Since there is
no farm at Send, there are no trainees who rise
especially early, although as a rule kitchen
workers are wakened slightly before the others.

After breakfast

3.82 Following breakfast trainees in both
institutions return to dormitories to change into
their work clothes (apart from schoolboys at Send)
and are marched dormitory by dormitory onto the
parade ground where they assemble into the various
parties. From there after roll check they proceed
to different work activities. At Send, since the
education staff do not begin until 9.00 am, the
morning school groups are drilled or have a
physical education session. There now follow
brief descriptions of the daytime activities.
Since the most obvious change is the introduction
of formal drill sessions, these will be described
first.

Drill

a. New Hall

3.83 Since September 1980 drill at New Hall has
taken place directly after lunch. Trainees are
dismissed from the dining hall, dormitory by
dormitory, at about 1.15 pm. Boots have to be put
on in the corridor, not in the dormitory, so for
about five minutes or so while everyone assembles
there is a great deal of noise and movement. Once
organised in bedspace order into two lines
stretching on each side of the exit door the
trainees are led out to form up outside in three
columns, standing easy. Most trainees will not
have had to hurry to make themselves ready for
there is ample time. But there are always those
who leave everything to the last moment and who
hop outside struggling with knotted laces or
unwilling boots. Apart from a few who murmur to
their friends or who shuffle to test the lacing of
their boots, most trainees stand motionless and
silent. Nobody is excused drill save those who
are due for release next day and who have to see
the probation officer and those who are medically
unfit (of this latter group those who are mobile
have to dress for drill and walk behind the main
body of trainees ready to be inspected).

3.84 As soon as it is certain that the number is
correct the word of command is given 'Squad! As
you were, as you were' (most trainees will have
been taken by surprise). 'Right, this time I want
to see those shoulders move, let's have a proper
brace up'. 'Squad - shun'. One hundred left feet
simultaneously are driven to the ground.

3.85 'By the left, quick march. Left right, left
right....' Most officers march the trainees out
at about 120 paces per minute and at this pace
they keep in step and co-ordinate surprisingly

well. The observer saw a few instances where a
much faster pace was called and this put quite a
lot of trainees out of step[12]. The squad moves on
to the parade ground. 'Squad, halt'. The
trainees halt. Almost all are still in step.
Those who are not are most likely to have been
receptions of the last couple of evenings, or else
the one or two trainees who seem unable to co-
ordinate no matter how much they practise. 'Left
turn'. The difference between those who know how
and those who do not becomes immediately obvious.

3.86 'Markers'. Three trainees march smartly
forward across the parade ground taking up their
positions. They turn to the left and stand to
attention. 'Parade - fall in'. The remaining
trainees break ranks, some marching, some walking
quickly towards their respective markers and, with
some assistance from the officer in charge, line
up to form three drill squads, each of three
ranks. All stand to attention.

3.87 'Dressing, right dress'. The markers remain
motionless but the remainder take one pace forward
and, except for those trainees in the second and
third ranks directly behind the markers, turn
their heads to the right and raise their right
arms behind the backs of the trainees to their
right. Once again the uninitiated can be easily
picked out as they glance uncertainly about them.
Trainees shuffle to adjust their position until
the correct spacing is achieved. Each trainee
should be able (without moving his head) to see
the chin of the man next but one. In this way
each rank should then be perfectly straight,
though in practice it rarely is. 'Eyes front'.

---

[12] The drill instructors are now more practised and it is
unlikely that this still occurs.

Heads turn sharply to the front and the right arms
are slapped smartly and noisily by the side.

3.88 'Open order march'. Trainees in the front
rank take one pace forward, those in the rear one
pace back. The dressing manoeuvre is repeated and
the parade should then be in open order ready for
inspection. In practice the officers move among
the trainees in an attempt to straighten the ranks
('Can you really see his chin'?) All trainees
should be standing properly to attention,
motionless and silent, heels together, the feet
turned out at an angle of 30°, arms held straight
by the sides, tucked in behind the hip bone, with
wrists straight, hands closed and thumbs extended
along the seams of the trousers, shoulders back,
chin tucked in, facing front with the eyes
directed forward and slightly upward. All
trainees are expected to remain motionless and
silent while they are inspected.

3.89 Each squad is inspected by one of the
officers responsible for it during the drill
session. He walks along the front rank halting
squarely in front of each trainee. He looks him
carefully up and down, sometimes adjusting a
jacket zip, a collar or a tie, sometimes advising
that some ill-fitting item of kit be changed at
the next opportunity or, more seriously, warning a
trainee to press his trousers before his next
appearance to avoid being put on report. He
passes more quickly back along the rear of each
rank pausing perhaps to straighten a trainee's
hunched shoulders or to comment on the backs of
any boots missed during cleaning.

3.90 Within the constraints set by the
availability of kit in prime condition the turnout
of most trainees on parade is very good and most
of the attention given by the inspecting officer
is to posture or merely to detail. Certainly

misbehaviour on the part of the trainees is very
rare indeed.

3.91 The inspection over, the command 'Close
order, march' is given. The trainees close ranks
and again it is obvious from the sound that most
trainees keep in time. The inspection is over and
some 10-15 minutes will have elapsed since the
trainees left the warmth of the detention centre
buildings.

3.92 The officers responsible for each squad then
take over command of their trainees 'A squad,
right turn, quick march'. 'A' squad marches from
the parade ground soon followed by 'B' squad.

3.93 'A' squad contains those trainees considered
more proficient at drill who have probably already
been at New Hall for several weeks and who have
achieved a sufficiently good standard to be
promoted. 'C' squad, on the other hand, contains
the newcomers and those who have not yet mastered
the basics of drill. 'B' squad consists of the
improvers, those who have accomplished the basics
and who are now trying to add co-ordination and
'polish' to their performance. Each squad will
contain 25 to 35 trainees. In fact on any
particular afternoon 'B' squad can be observed to
perform as well as or better than 'A' squad and it
is not unusual for a trainee to be demoted, either
for consistently poor performance, apparent lack
of effort, or non co-operation. To most trainees
demotion is something to be avoided just as
promotion is something they strive for.

3.94 'C' squad remains on the parade square to
practise the basics of coming to attention,
standing at ease, open and close order march,
dressing, marching and turning. Careful attention
is paid to the correctness of each movement.
Knees have to be raised until the thigh is

parallel to the ground. The right leg has to remain straight when marching into open or close order. Timing is stressed too and in the early stages trainees are encouraged to call out the time loudly: 'One - two three - one' echoes across the surrounding countryside. Some months after the start of the pilot project the Prison Service Drill Manual was published and this helped considerably. Before that time the teaching of drill at New Hall was beset by minor differences in the movements required by each officer, differences reflecting his own particular service experience.

3.95 Within 'C' squad those trainees who have arrived within the previous couple of days are taken to one side by an officer to be given closer and more basic instruction.

3.96 Throughout drill the emphasis is on a proper instruction and on the standard of performance achieved by each squad. As with other aspects of the new regime the intention is not to make the experience punitive, demoralising or physically exhausting. Most officers show commendable patience and if necessary demonstrate and explain particular moves repeatedly. Even so, their approach puts pressure on trainees to learn and learn fast and most trainees genuinely try to improve. As with other activities officers differ in personal approach. All will swiftly penalise obvious lack of effort, but while the trainee genuinely experiencing difficulty may be treated patiently and quite sympathetically by one officer he may be given a sharp lecture on idleness by another.

3.97 'A' squad normally drills on the basketball pitch, to which it has been marched immediately the parade is over. Here the emphasis is on marching, wheeling, turning right and left and turning about on the march, paying particular attention to dressing. The practice is physically more demanding than that for 'C' squad but is well within the capacity of the average trainee. If the session goes well the squad can go on to practise sequence drill, but the area available is inadequate for this and much better suited to wheeling and turning.

3.98 'B' squad is drilled on the roadway leading up to the basketball pitch. This roadway is narrow and sloping with a 40° bend at its midpoint, so it is far from ideal for drill. 'B' squad pounds up and down this short stretch of roadway, backwards and forwards for almost the entire period. The space available allows the officer to concentrate on only basic foot drill, marching, turning about on the march, and maintaining proper dressing.

3.99 A regulation five minute break is included about mid-way through the period during which trainees stand easy, and attend to the re-tying of bootlaces or the blowing of noses. Some officers use this period to comment on the squad's performance or to demonstrate again any moves which seem particularly troublesome. Others carefully time the period and re-start the moment the specified time has elapsed.

3.100 At the end of the period all three squads march back to the entrance to the corridor independently and enter in single file. They have to change and re-group for the next period of PE or work by 2.30 pm so the changing time involved usually removes about 5-10 minutes from the end of the hour set aside for drill. In effect, between the end of the parade and returning to the dormitory to change, a maximum of 40 minutes has been spent at drill. Most trainees appear to have enjoyed this period to some extent or at least to have preferred it to work.

3.101 One further factor limits drill: the weather. In September 1980 the warden consulted Regional Office on the subject of drill in adverse weather conditions and on the possibility of obtaining suitable protective clothing. He was advised that drill should continue in the lightest rainfall and certainly not in conditions of moderate rainfall likely to cause the trainees' normal clothing to get really wet. This advice was adopted as local policy in October 1980 and has been adhered to since that time.

3.102 When the new regime was introduced it was intended that chopping and sawing logs would serve, at New Hall, as a physically demanding, wet weather alternative to work. In fact this alternative has been employed on only a few occasions and it is normal practice during wet weather for trainees to return to their normal work parties instead.

b.   **Send**

3.103 Prior to the commencement of the new regime, there were no formal drill sessions in the programme. The inmates were not marched from one activity to another: they were escorted in groups by an officer in what was called walking smartly to distinguish it from marching. Since 21 April 1980, there have been formal drill sessions under the supervision of an officer, totalling 70 minutes per day for nearly all trainees. All the discipline staff are involved in drill training. For some of them drilling a column of boys comes more easily than for others. Approximately 35% of the officers have come from the armed services, a traditional recruiting catchment for the prison service. The manoeuvres

performed by the column (up to 15 in all) are
simple in comparison with those performed by
soldiers in ceremonial, but given the limitations
of many of the trainees and the short period
available in the sentence, simplicity is
appropriate. Among the movements the trainees
learn are: how to stand at attention; to march,
starting from the left foot in unison, swinging
their arms, in time with the step, from the
shoulder; to left and right wheel; to mark time;
and to stop together.

3.104 Initially the attempts of the new trainees
are comical, arousing derision and suppressed
merriment from the more experienced trainees.
However, expression of these natural outbreaks is
quickly controlled. For most of the trainees,
drilling appears to be an enjoyable period. They
quickly learn to approximate the movements, but
there are always some who manoeuvre in the wrong
direction.

3.105 To describe the officers as patient with the
trainees makes them sound too passive: however,
for the most part trainees are taught how to
drill, not bullied into conformity. Drilling
takes place in all but the most inclement weather
and on rainy days, long waterproofs are worn. The
drill, involving as it does complete supervision
on the parade square, has had the general effect
of improving the appearance of the trainees. The
trainees who are young adolescents are a mixture
of shapes and sizes. Because Send is a small
institution it could not carry sufficient range of
kit to ensure that all these could be properly
fitted at all times and therefore not infrequently
during the period of observation boys were issued
with ill-fitting clothes for up to a week before
the correct size could be obtained. This
inevitably detracted from the smartness of the
drill session.

Work

a.   **Send**

3.106 Before the implementation of the changed
regime there was one workshop where boys broke up
faulty cassettes. It was considered that such
work was inappropriate to the new character of
Send in that it was difficult to set a pace and
after a time trainees became apathetic. The
workshop was converted to a supplementary
gymnasium. Work at the centre falls into two
categories: maintaining and running the
institution and market garden work. The major
activities are described below, in rough ascending
order starting with the one trainees least prefer.

i.   **Market gardens**

3.107 The market gardens cover an area of four and
a half hectares. They are located within the
perimeter fence, and contain 17 polythene tunnels,
as well as the outdoor growing area. Cabbage,
lettuce, tomatoes, cucumbers and root vegetables
are the major crops. Bedding plants for the
gardens surrounding the more public areas of the
centre are also produced. The work is organised
by four officer instructors and this supervision
is supplemented by discipline officers, their
number determined by how many trainees are working
together. In addition boys work on the ornamental
flower beds surrounding the main buildings.
Although many of the trainees experience the work
as uncomfortable this depends on the season and
the point reached in the growing cycle, so in that
sense its 'hardness' varies.

3.108 In the winter the trainees complain about
the field work and in summer they dislike working
in the tunnels which can become hot and humid. It
is useful work in that the centre consumes its own

produce and some of it goes to feed other establishments in the system.

3.109 Close supervision is required because, with the rapid turnover of trainees, they inevitably do not have the satisfaction of seeing their work come to fruition. Consequently planting becomes merely sticking seedlings into soil and the digging merely turning over dirt. Since they only see one stage of the growing process they develop no sense of responsibility towards the plants or to the fabric of the tunnels. Most of the little vandalism that occurred during the period of observation in the centre happened here, occasionally a spade or fork piercing the polythene fabric 'inadvertently'. On windy days this can be fairly damaging and it is hard to locate the culprit or to sort out accidents from malicious damage. This is true also of the flower beds, although since responsibility is more easily attributable, vandalism is less, though interest is no greater. On occasions when trainees who were weeding were asked if they could distinguish the plants from the weeds the reply was 'No, I was told to pull out these ones'! Thus an activity which provides recreation for many of the inhabitants of Surrey on a fine summer's day is merely another chore for the trainees.

3.110 Many of the boys are from inner city areas and have had no contact with farm life[13]. The chore universally greeted with horror is manuring the rows of plants. At one corner of the great field there is a large manure heap which is from time to time dug out and transported in hand carts to spread between the rows. This chore is

---

[13] Since the change in Send's catchment area in 1981 many more of the receptions are from rural areas.

executed with delicacy by the majority of the boys, who take inordinate care that no muck should attach itself either to their spade handles or to their clothes. One was heard to question whether the television cameras could film this and another to wonder what the public would say if they knew what trainees were made to do at Send. It is a nice illustration of how difficult it is to predict which aspects of the regime trainees will find rigorous.

3.111 When horticultural work was slack this party was given the task of sawing logs. While the logs could be sold, the venture was hardly economic. The intention behind the introduction of this activity was to provide 'demanding' work when other such work was not available. In that, it was the nearest a modern establishment came to the treadmill. It was an innovation of the new regime. It took place inside a polythene tunnel which was lying fallow, the logs being placed on smart new carpentry benches. When the logging was in progress, there was quite an amount of wood dust in the confined space which was unpleasant. The staff had mixed feelings about it, some feeling that this hard work had something of the old detention centres about it, others viewing the new benches ironically. More recently it has been possible to organise the work so that it has not been necessary to occupy the boys at logging.

ii.   **Maintenance**

3.112 Apart from cleaning and the upkeep of the decorative flower beds around the centre it is, as in all institutions, a major task to maintain the fabric of the place. Much of the minor building is carried out by the works department under the supervision of the senior works officer and his staff. The conversion of the workshop to a

gymnasium, extensions to the stores and provision
of a staff mess as well as maintenance of staff
quarters have been carried out by this department
with the help of trainees labour. Generally the
technical work is done by the trades officers, the
trainees being useful only for the labouring
tasks. Work outside the fence - whether on
maintenance or the outside garden party - is only
carried out by those trainees who have been
security cleared and who have reached the second
grade. Certain offence categories are precluded,
for example those who have a conviction for a sex
offence, however minor, are not permitted outside.
The one incident of absconding from Send during
the period of observation occurred from the
outside garden party. He was recaptured within
one hour by a member of staff within a mile of the
institution, and appeared before the Board of
Visitors for absconding.

iii. **Small laundry**

3.113 Work here is not highly sought after by the
trainees. The work is hard, the laundry becomes
hot and steamy and the inmates are under very
close supervision by the laundress. All of the
centre uniforms are washed here, as well as the
clothes the boys had' when they arrived at
reception.

iv. **Kitchen**

3.114 The kitchen is not large but it is well
equipped and professionally organised. Kitchen
work, as in all penal establishments, is something
of a prize. It is hard but sociable. Although
tightly run, the discipline is that inherent in
providing regular meals on time for a large number
of trainees and has therefore, an obvious purpose.
The catering officer and his relief officer work
alongside the trainees, as chef with his

assistants. Everything is spotlessly clean. The
nature of the work includes a strong element of
training and this has been formalised into a
catering certificate under the aegis of the
education department. The boy can take this with
him when he leaves. Although because of the
shortness of the sentence this will not suffice as
a catering qualification outside, it at least
provides some boys with an appropriate
introduction to the trade. Since it is important
for the smooth running of the kitchen, all of the
trainees who work here are over school leaving
age. However, as is the nature of these things,
the proportion of such trainees in the centre
fluctuates and sometimes the kitchen is under
great pressure due to shortage of labour.
Schoolboys are not permitted to work in the
kitchen. The kitchen party drills separately and
their physical education classes are programmed to
fit the meal time deadlines. This and their
access to the best of the food creates something
of an elite group. It proves too much temptation,
however, for some boys, and a degree of vigilance
is necessary to prevent removal of foodstuffs from
the kitchen. In the close discipline of Send this
is a serious offence and the penalties include
loss of remission. It must be remembered that in
all institutions goods become currency. In adult
prisons tobacco is the major currency. At Send,
where they are not allowed to smoke, the trainees
attempt to trade in food and sweets. (The Mars
bar is the standard unit of currency). This trade
is fairly successfully checked at Send, where the
officers keep a special vigilance at meal times
and over the trainees' lockers to ensure, as far
as possible, that younger or weaker trainees are
not 'persuaded' to give up their food or sweets.

v.   Orderlies

3.115 At the gate, in reception, in the education
and administration departments, in the stores and
in the officers' mess there are orderlies whose
task it is to keep the places clean and to assist
those departments. Apart from the mess boy, who
has access to a tea-kettle, there are few concrete
advantages to these jobs. Orderlies are always in
the second and third grade. Although they have
laid down job descriptions, they know that they
hold positions of trust and are not supervised as
closely as other trainees. These jobs are prized
and relations with supervisors are at their most
friendly. The work does not appear heavy but all
orderlies are subject to drill and the extra PE.

3.116 This is but an incomplete sketch of the work
trainees do at Send. The work is seldom
backbreaking and is often useful. It rarely has
any elements which would translate easily to a
skill relevant in the city to which most of the
boys at the time returned, but it is hard to
imagine how that could be achieved in the short
span of the sentence. It is seldom drudgery and
for the most part work is not much resented.
Sometimes there is light relief and occasionally
the tasks themselves are satisfying, as in the
kitchen. However, fights do occasionally break
out at work and given the tools used in gardens
and in the kitchen, this could be serious. That
there was never a serious injury during the period
of observation at Send is a tribute to the
vigilance of the staff.

Work

b.   New Hall

3.117 The work available at New Hall is more
varied. In addition to the activities at Send

(orderlies, cleaners, market gardens, decorative
gardens, engineers and kitchen) there is also a
dairy farm, piggery and loom shop. Although party
organisation is rather different, the descriptions
of work at Send are adequate to give a flavour of
how it is performed at New Hall. The following
sections describe those parties which are unique
to New Hall.

i.   **Dairy**

3.118 Trainees who work in the dairy rise much
earlier than the rest of the population (at about
5.30 am). Under the supervision of the farm
manager and agricultural craftsman, they are
responsible for a herd of about 80 cows. This
involves milking them morning and evening,
cleaning them out and feeding them as well as
looking after those calves which are retained to
improve the stock. Although supervised,
considerable responsibility rests on these
trainees and there is quite a lot to learn. Many,
though not all, find the work interesting and they
work conscientiously despite the long hours.
Those who do not soon lose their places on the
party. Because of the risks which would stem from
poor workmanship the emphasis here is on
encouraging the trainees to take an interest, and
on working efficiently to get everything done in
the available time. The trainees often work
alongside staff, at other times they work alone,
but throughout the long day there is little slack
time.

3.119 The coming of the new regime carried a
number of problems for this party. Drill and
extra PE reduced working hours and led at first to
some workings days being very disrupted.
Amendments to the timetable which were introduced
in September 1980 resolved some of these problems.
The disappearance of trainees with six month

sentences made it difficult to retain a core of
experienced trainees, and made the proposed
proficiency testing impractical.

ii.   Piggery

3.120 Under direction trainees are responsible for
feeding and cleaning out the large stock of
breeding sows and weaner piglets. The hours are
not as long as on the dairy party and none of the
work carries the same urgency as milking but it is
still interesting and the supervision less close
than on most parties.

iii. General farm party

3.121 This party varies in size according to
season. At harvest time there is much hard work
to be done gathering, loading and stacking bales
of hay. For much of the time there is a steady
round of digging out ditches, keeping culverts
clear, cutting hedges and generally keeping the
200 acres of estate workable and safe. In summer,
despite the hard work involved, allocation to this
party can give welcome relief from the closeness
of the centre, since the day's task can be almost
half a mile away across the fields out of sight of
the buildings. The experience in winter can be in
harsh contrast. Pouring rain or driving snow
makes the party a much less attractive proposition
for trainees and staff alike.

iv.   Loom shop

3.122 Normally 16 trainees working in pairs
operate hand looms weaving bed rugs for use in
penal establishments. Operating the looms is
physically demanding and unremitting work which
can raise blisters within minutes on the soft
hands of the new trainee. Some skill and
dexterity is required if the loom is to be

operated efficiently but most find this repetitive
job boring. A reasonably good standard and a
relatively high rate of production are required.
Prior to the introduction of the new regime the
daily target per loom was 20 yards of material per
day, at nine passes of the shuttle per inch.
Under the new time-table the production target was
reduced to 5 x 84 inch bed rugs per day. By
working trainees in pairs, one operating the loom
and the other preparing shuttles, the work can be
punctuated by rest periods. 'Tying off' sessions
are easier but not very interesting.

3.123 Under the new regime in New Hall few changes
were made to the nature of the work performed.
However, there was an expectation of greater
effort by the trainee to compensate for the
reduction in working hours. Unlike at Send drill
time came entirely out of the working day. There
was evidence of a fall in output after the
introduction of the new regime.

Education

a.   **Send**

3.124 As a junior detention centre, because of the
requirement to provide full time education for
those of school age, this is a major department.
The department also runs a library, an important
facility in an institution where there is little
association, and where television is very limited.

3.125 When the pilot project was introduced at
Send education time was cut (while still meeting
the legal requirement) and the curriculum
restricted in scope, those subjects considered
incompatible with the tougher regime being
dropped. During the period of observation about
three quarters of the boys at Send were of school

age[14] and about a quarter of the population were in need of remedial education. The complement of the education department was reduced by one part-time teacher (to five full-time and five part-time staff) after the implementation of the new regime, but the number of hours worked by the part-time teachers fell because there were fewer daytime hours in the education programme.

3.126 The morning classes start at 9.00 am and finish at 12.15 pm with a 15 minute break at 10.15 am. The afternoon begins at 1.30 pm and finishes at 4.15 pm with a 15 minute drill period. The evening classes commence at 6.00 pm and stop at 8.00 pm. The boys are divided into groups, up to 10 in all, to ensure that they all receive the required education time while fulfilling the work and drill requirements. Before April 1980 trainees were streamed into ability groups. Often this has not happened subsequently because low rolls have meant that it would not be economical to split very small classes for this reason. One effect has been that there has been more teaching at an individual level.

3.127 The educational background of the trainees (many of whom will have been truants from school) and the rapid turnover causes particular problems for the education staff. Some of them told the observer they would prefer a curriculum which involved less duplication of the kind of education in which many of the boys had already failed, although others did not share this view.

---

[14] The proportion has since declined to nearer a half.

b.   **New Hall**

3.128 In a senior detention centre education does
not feature so prominently in the regime. Daytime
classes are limited to providing remedial basic
education, and maintenance classes for the
occasional trainee continuing a course of further
education. The main educational provision is in
the evening.

3.129 All trainees undergo educational and
intelligence testing on arrival and under the
previous regime all of those with reading ages
below 10.5 years received remedial education (113
out of 497 receptions during 1979). Three classes
used to be held each day but under the new regime
this was reduced to two operating only in the
morning. In practice, therefore, remedial
education was restricted to the most needy 15
trainees, a marginal reduction. Within the
classroom the atmosphere is purposeful though
strict. Discipline is neither evident nor
necessary most of the time. The emphasis is on
developing confidence and communication skills,
not just on basic reading and writing. A friendly
classroom atmosphere and individual attention is
considered conducive to achieving this aim.

3.130 All trainees attend evening classes on four
evenings of the week. The evening provision is
designed to offer a balanced programme of formal
education and interest activities as well as
practical classes related to the demands of
everyday life: basic cooking, parent-craft, job-
search, first aid etc. Following the introduction
of the new regime the cycle of classes was changed
to a four week as opposed to an eight week one
since the programme now had to cater exclusively
for those serving a three month sentence. Also
the style of the classes changed somewhat. Art
and craft classes became more craft oriented as

more befitting the new ethos; for instance metalwork was substituted for painting.

3.131 The skilled labourers course designed to develop the basic skills required of a building labourer, and catering normally for up to eight trainees, was closed. Its length was considered incompatible with the shorter sentences and its pace was reckoned to be inconsistent with the intended briskness of the new regime.

3.132 Under the new regime, occasional trainees already involved in day release courses continued to be allowed study leave during sentence and to be granted day release to attend college. It was considered important that trainees should not lose their places through enforced non-attendance.

Physical education: Send and New Hall

3.133 Although all the trainees have been medically passed for the tougher regime, some find physical education especially hard in the beginning. The emphasis is more on activities like circuit training, weight training, gymnastics and running than on the teaching of physical skills and fitness. The PE instructors are able to motivate the trainees most of the time. All work is done in groups, and occasionally trainees can be seen trying to stay outside the gaze of the instructor in order to get away with doing fewer press-ups or bar curls. The officers are soon aware of those who are slacking and they are simply made to repeat the exercise. Each trainee's progress is measured against his original performance recorded on his card, and most trainees are pleased to take their record card away with them at the end of their sentence, noting with satisfaction that their performance has improved.

The remainder of the sentence: Send and New Hall

3.134 Provided he has lost no remission through misbehaviour the trainee can expect to be released after about 46 days from the junior centre and after about 60 days from the senior centre[15].

3.135 Discharge procedures begin a fortnight before release. The trainee's street clothing is checked in his presence by the warden or his deputy and supplemented where necessary. Some days before discharge the trainee again sees the warden who explains the terms of the supervision licence. Together they sign it. If the Firearms Act 1968 is relevant, this is explained and again both sign the notification document. The centre knows the boys who will be picked up by their parents on the morning of discharge. Those who are to travel by public transport have their warrant, subsistence, and route home explained, and are driven to the station.

CONCLUSION

3.136 After the Home Secretary's announcement in October 1979 of the pilot project there had been much speculation about the form which the initiative would take. The new regimes as defined in the Note of Guidance avoided, and in fact safe-guarded against, punitive extremes. The intention was to modify the existing programmes in a number of ways to ensure a brisker pace under close

---

[15] Part I of the Criminal Justice Act 1982 was implemented on 24 May 1983. Since that date all detention centres, including Send and New Hall, have taken trainees with sentences ranging between three weeks and four months. All detention centre sentences are now reduced by remand time spent in custody and attract one-third remission.

supervision, but not to put at risk the reasonably good relationship that existed between staff and trainees.

3.137 It had been recognised that there would be variation between the two centres because of the different age groups and facilities in each place. The observers were left with the impression, certainly at the beginning, that the pilot regime operated better in Send than in New Hall. However, in neither institution was the regime change dramatic since many of the features sought by the Home Secretary were already present in each. Parades and inspections were already central features of the regimes and the standards of personal hygiene and appearance and of cleanliness and tidiness of the accommodation were already very high.

3.138 It is true that the number of parades was increased, as was the amount of kit to be maintained and prepared for inspections, but the effect was marginally to heighten the emphasis of these parts of the programme rather than to increase their impact significantly. Formal drill was new, although it had been a feature of the early detention centre regimes and vestiges remained in operation at New Hall and at Send: trainees 'walked smartly' rather than marched from place to place with the requirement that they kept in formation but with no across-the-board insistence that they remain completely in step. When going on parade or arriving outside the dining hall they would mark time until told to halt and a number of military words of command were still employed.

3.139 The inclusion of drill as a regular feature of the regime had three immediate but varying effects in each institution. In both places, it introduced a new element into the trainee's day in

which he was subject to close instruction and 100%
surveillance by an officer, an element which
required of him continuous effort and attention.
Secondly, in both institutions it had the effect
of injecting more polish into movement about the
centre, inspections and parades. Thirdly, the
time allocated to drill and extra PE entailed a
reduction (although because of other timetabling
changes not a corresponding one) in that available
for other activities. At New Hall these extra
elements in the programme had to come very largely
out of the working day, and this was a major cause
of dissatisfaction with the new regime among the
staff there.

3.140 At the junior detention centre the daily
schedule had an added element: daytime education
for the majority of trainees. The extra PE was
accommodated by the device of including some of
the PE programme in the evening but most of it in
the daytime programme in such a way as to reduce
the amount of time trainees spent in the
classroom. Overall the amount of time allocated
to work was unchanged. However, unlike at New
Hall where after September 1980 the whole
population drilled at the same time, at Send drill
was timetabled for most trainees in small groups
and in three short daily sessions. The effect of
including PE and drill in the day-time programme
in this way was to increase considerably the
amount of movement about the institution. This
fragmentation of the day meant that the time spent
on any one activity was slightly reduced owing to
the logistics of moving from place to place. It
nevertheless contributed to the general air of an
institution humming with activity. The staff at
Send were more likely to recognise that the tempo
of the centre had improved. Consequently there
were few among the discipline grades who wished to
see a significant reduction in the new elements

(drill and extra PE) but many would have preferred a solution which further reduced the time spent in education.

3.141 Trainees always did have to earn their limited privileges by good behaviour and also by effort. The main change in this direction was to make privileges more limited. At New Hall only comparatively rarely since the new regime was introduced have grade twos had an opportunity of playing table tennis or darts during their short period of evening association. At Send the limitations have included the loss for grade threes of their privilege television. Another stimulus to do well, the evening PE award schemes, was lost not because it was considered incompatible with the new regime but because it could no longer be fitted into the timetable. The effect of the contraction of the range of privileges on incentives has been more noticeable at New Hall than at Send. But the feeling central to grade promotion - of having succeeded and of not having been left behind by the others - remains.

3.142 In giving an account of the regime observation undertaken at Send and New Hall, this chapter has sought to summarise the changes that were made when the pilot project started, to describe a number of institutional routines and to reach tentative conclusions about the implementation of the new regime. As the preceding pages show, the required changes in routine were put into effect in both Send and New Hall and for the most part have been faithfully retained without significant erosion. Other parts of the routine were not intended to change and so much of the regime remained the same and broadly felt the same to the observers. The conclusions about whether the regime was indeed brisker, harder physically, and generally more demanding

cannot easily be taken independently of the close
perceptions of the separate parts of the regime
described in the second half of this chapter. But
it is worth drawing out the general direction of
those conclusions. When one considers the quality
of the staff-trainee interactions in drill,
physical education, work, education and in the
general supervision of cleaning dormitories and
preparing for work, parades and inspections the
picture is an uneven one. However, physical
education was made more strenuous, some effort was
made to inject pace into the domestic chores and
some work parties, and the introduction of drill
contributed to making the regime brisker.
Overall, the regime appeared busier and demands
and close supervision were a little more
prominent. It is also clear that in other areas
(for example, in others of the work parties and in
education) there was little movement in these
respects. Paradoxically, however, at the same
time that efforts were being made to inject
brisker and more demanding requirements there was
a counter-balancing feature. The various areas in
which it was feasible to be more demanding also
seem to have been more stimulating. An officer
who exercised stricter control of his trainees in
drill, for example, might also have been the one
to employ a patient modelling approach in teaching
drill. So it was more possible for a positive
staff-trainee interaction to thrive than, for
example, within the more continuous chore of a
humdrum work party on which the officer might have
had little choice but to be altogether less
active. In this respect the requirement not to
put at risk good staff-trainee relationships seems
to have been amply met. So the reduction in
continuous monotony of tasks and the fragmentation
brought about by the new timetable at least seems
to have counter-balanced the attempts to make
things stricter and more demanding. In some
instances it actually led to a more varied
existence in which the time passed more quickly.

4.   STAFF SURVEYS

INTRODUCTION

4.1   Two surveys of staff views were conducted at
Send and New Hall. The first was planned for
Autumn 1980, only a few months after the
introduction of the new regime, with the aim of
ascertaining staff reaction to the nature of the
changes and their implementation, as well as their
opinions about the immediate impact on the two
establishments. The second survey was carried out
during September and October 1982 to canvass the
opinion of staff about the operation of the new
regime once it had had time to settle down.

4.2   It was recognised from the outset that it was
important to survey staff opinion in this way: it
is the staff who are responsible for the final
practical stage of putting policy into effect;
they see directly how trainees respond to the
regime; and they personally experience the degree
of co-operation or resistance with which the
various activities are met. The staff surveys
also reveal something of the impact upon the staff
themselves.

4.3   This chapter presents the main findings of
these surveys, together with a brief discussion of
what may be inferred from them.

THE FIRST STAFF SURVEY

4.4   Interviewing was selected as the most fitting
method in the circumstances. It was felt that the
imposition of a questionnaire would have been
unduly restrictive, since staff were willing to
express their views freely. Despite the risk of
interviewer bias and the considerable amount of
time required for such interviews there were

thought to be a number of advantages: few
refusals, fuller replies representing the person's
own views rather than the 'party line', and an
altogether more flexible approach.

4.5   The psychologists attached to observe the two
detention centres conducted both surveys. The
staff were thus well acquainted with the
interviewers and were well known to them, and the
interviewers were, themselves, familiar with the
day-to-day workings of the detention centres.

4.6   The first staff were seen at the beginning of
October 1980 and all but one of the interviews
were completed by the end of the year. At New
Hall there were no refusals and at Send all but
three of those approached agreed to take part.

4.7   The interviews were built around a series of
open-ended questions about the regime and the
changes that had taken place. Each of these
questions was more in the nature of a stimulus
intended to elicit a full expression of opinion
rather than a specific question requiring a
definitive response. Each member of staff was
interviewed individually, each interview lasting
approximately three quarters of an hour (although
some took considerably longer). Transcripts were
made of the replies, most of which were word-for-
word. The summaries presented in this chapter aim
to convey the range of opinion and the degree of
consensus about particular issues. Guarantees of
confidentiality were given to staff.

At New Hall

4.8   Forty five members of staff were interviewed
at New Hall. This represented the vast majority
of staff having daily contact with trainees
(warden, deputy warden, most discipline staff,
hospital officers, most members of the works

staff, PE instructors, most of the farm and
gardens staff, education officer, one of the
probation officers and the storeman).

4.9 Drill and PE were seen by staff as the
central elements around which the new timetable
had been built. By contrast, few referred to the
other intended changes (shorter association time,
earlier lights out, ensuring that trainees were
always visibly occupied etc). Two thirds of those
questioned felt that the emphasis within the
regime on work had been reduced through shorter
working hours or loss of continuity at work and
regarded this as one of the main changes.
However, many made it clear that they saw this as
an unwelcome side effect of introducing drill and
extra PE rather than as a primary intention.

4.10 Twelve of those interviewed said that they
believed drill to be a good and important addition
to the regime and five others thought its
usefulness was limited to the first week or two.
By contrast 15 considered drill to be of little or
no value and 10 thought its introduction actually
had been counter-productive. Three others argued
that drill would have been important and valuable
'if it had been done properly'. On balance,
therefore, the majority of staff (33 out of the 45
interviewed) did not, at that time, consider the
drill to be worthwhile as a major element in the
regime.

4.11 Although there was no criticism of the
instructors, who were almost universally
acknowledged to be doing a good job, the great
majority of the New Hall staff felt that the extra
PE was either unimportant (30) or counter-
productive (8). Most were against reducing the
trainees' working week simply to accommodate what
many viewed as recreation.

4.12 Ideas about the value of work itself varied.
Several emphasised the training value of some of
the work and regretted the shorter work sessions
and the closure of the construction industry
course. Some suggested that continuous hard work
was what trainees disliked and that, therefore,
this kind of activity should hold a central
position in a deterrent regime. Others reconciled
the trainees' presumed dislike of long work
periods and the supposed training value by talking
of establishing regular work patterns or the work
habit. Of course, there can be no single,
definitive view as to the value of work and it
would be wrong to assume that all trainees possess
the same attitude towards work and reluctance to
do it. No doubt, many of the differences in
opinion reflected the member of staff's own
experience of supervising trainees at work.
Officers who regularly supervise the completion of
the more monotonous cleaning or digging tasks may
tend to make observations which implicitly
subscribe to a 'deterrent theory' whereas trades
officers and civilian workmen working with one or
two regular, selected trainees on more skilled
tasks would focus on the training value of the
experience. None of those questioned at New Hall
felt that the changes had resulted in the improved
running of the centre; most (34) claimed there had
been a general deterioration. Areas mentioned in
this deterioration were work, standards in
cleaning parties, staff morale and a loss in
discipline and control. The only areas where any
staff thought there might have been an improvement
were the briskness of the day (suggested by two
officers), discipline (2), efficiency (1) and
smartness (1).

4.13 A minority (12) of the New Hall staff liked
working under the new system, most were relatively
non-committal (17) or expressed dislike (16).
Specific dislikes included what was seen as the

futility and cosmetic value of the new regime,
drill and the perceived adverse effect of its
introduction upon work, and a decrease in staff
morale.

4.14 A few felt that their job had become easier
(7) and this was primarily because of shortened
work periods and the consequent relief from the
tedium of supervising outside work parties. The
majority opinion, held by just over half of those
interviewed (24), was that the job had become more
difficult. The views were varied and tended to
reflect the differing nature of their
responsibilities. Drill was mentioned as an
additional and demanding task, unwelcome to some.
Those in administrative positions complained of
being more desk-bound since, for example, the
detailing was more complicated because of the need
to programme in extra activities. Works staff
pointed out that the reduction in trainees'
working time placed a greater burden on them and
required more care and effort in organising use of
the time remaining. Finally, several noted that
the task of controlling trainees had become more
difficult both because of the need to get the
trainees to work harder to get the work done in
the shorter time, and because the trainees
themselves seemed less co-operative.

4.15 The majority (37) felt that there was some
conflict between staff and that, among discipline
officers, this related mainly to drill.
Contention centred on detailing to the task and
what were seen as inconsistencies in the methods
and approach to be adopted on the drill square, as
well as on different views as to the value of
drill in the regime. The strength of feeling was
fuelled to some extent by the fact that drill was
perceived as a new, demanding and, for many,
threatening task. Experience suggests that staff
generally report conflict and that such opinions

might be obtained in any other establishment
whether or not there had been a change in the
organisation or regime. In fact, 10 of the staff
made this point, suggesting that conflict is
almost inevitable between groups which may be
working toward differing objectives. Others,
recognising this feature of institutions,
nevertheless maintained that the introduction of
the new regime had amplified this process. At
this stage, four to six months after the new
regime had been introduced, only seven maintained
that the staff were 'pulling together'.

4.16 The staff assessment of the effect of the new
regime on the trainees was not unanimous: a third
of those replying had no definite view, choosing
instead to comment on the trainees' immediate
reaction to the regime; four volunteered that
trainees were now fitter; eight saw improvements
of other sorts such as smarter appearance; and
eight noted adverse effects such as a
deterioration in trainee behaviour, a loss of
alertness, increased disciplinary offences or
increased bravado. Overall it is probably fair to
conclude from the replies that few staff at this
early stage confidently would have predicted any
lasting effect for the new regime. Even amongst
those pointing to improvements, most reports were
of relatively incidental advances which might be
only short-lived such as smarter appearance or
increased physical fitness.

4.17 Almost three quarters (33) of those
interviewed stated that the trainees now found the
regime easier than previously. Seven claimed that
it was now harder but four of these added that
this held only for the first week or two after
which most trainees found the new regime
relatively easy. Those who felt that trainees now
found the regime easier considered that this was

because they were spending a greater proportion of their time on things they enjoyed, had some respite from work due to the new time-tabling, and because the extra variety in activities helped make the time pass more quickly. Thirty members of staff thought the regime had become more interesting (or rather less boring) for this reason although some of them also maintained that there was less value in the new regime since what few training opportunities there were had been curtailed. The most difficult part of the sentence was seen as being the first two or three weeks in which the trainee has to adjust to the demands of the regime. Drill was seen as adding something to this demand at this initial stage but, in general, the regime was not viewed as having changed materially in so far as it affected trainees.

4.18 Staff largely agreed (32) that trainees were now worse behaved than previously. Two thought that behaviour had improved and 11 that it had not changed. Several suggestions were advanced to account for this: trainees were different now due to the change in catchment area[1], poorer control, lower standards of discipline within the centre, and cyclical changes - the idea that trainee behaviour follows a kind of cyclical trend, tranquil periods being succeeded by periods of disturbance.

4.19 Because of concern that a toughening of the regime might possibly damage the quality of the relationship between staff and trainees, and because it was the specific intention to safeguard this aspect of life in detention centres, items

---

[1] The catchment area for New Hall was changed in February 1980 (see paragraph 2.39 above).

about the quality of relationships were included in the interview schedule.

4.20 Although two thirds of those interviewed agreed that the quality of the relationships they had established with trainees had not suffered as a result of the new regime, 14 reported deterioration of some sort. Various reasons were put forward for this including the disappearance from New Hall of the six monthers, and limited opportunity to establish a relationship due to the shorter work periods and reduced association time. Some pointed to deteriorating relations rather than eroded relationships. In this connection it was clear that the word 'relationship' can be interpreted in two distinct though related ways: first in terms of human relationship (mutual acceptance and personal communication - as most people choose to use the word) but secondly in terms of the more formal relationship between the roles of the two individuals or groups. In this sense it had much to do with trainee respect and deference to the officer's authority.

4.21 The majority of staff (26) reported that their handling of the inmates had not changed. Many of these claimed that there was only one way to handle trainees in order to get the best out of them and that was to be 'firm but fair', to state clearly what was required and to insist upon good performance, yet always to be ready to listen to a trainee's complaints and to help him when required. Eleven staff said they were now stricter, and six less strict, with trainees.

4.22 During the preceding period staff had been exposed to a spirited public debate and much speculation within the media about the likely nature and effect of the new regime. Indeed there had been much speculation among the staff themselves. Consequently questions were put to

the staff about the expectations they had formed
following the Home Secretary's speech to the
Conservative and Unionist Party conference in
October 1979, and the ensuing public debate. It
should be emphasised that this was not an exercise
in conjecture but was rather an attempt to assess
the extent of any divergence between what the
staff had come to expect and the regime that had
been implemented. The most commonly held view
(24) was that something far more strict and tough
had been expected, more along the lines of the
army 'glass-house' of yesteryear. The regime that
had been established contained the expected
elements but only in what some saw as a mild,
emasculated form. Their view was that New Hall's
regime was not a short, sharp, shock, not a
deterrent, and not what the media coverage had led
them to expect. However, 16 felt that the regime
broadly matched up to their initial expectations
and that anything more tough would have required
changes in legislation or would have proved
unacceptable in a modern civilised society.

4.23 Just over half of those interviewed (27) felt
that New Hall was not being used for the right
sort of trainee, 11 were broadly satisfied with
those received and seven did not express a view.
The most common view was that the regime was most
suitable for those at an early stage in their
criminal careers (17) whilst, it was supposed,
they were relatively impressionable.

4.24 Seven staff were satisfied with, and 27 were
critical of, the way in which the new regime had
been planned and implemented. Criticisms varied
but many of them centred around a view that the
process had been insufficiently informed by a
knowledge of the realities of detention centre
life and that the timescale had been too short to
allow adequate preparation. Thirty-three
maintained that the views of those who worked in

detention centres had not been adequately taken
into account. A number considered that there had
been too little training for the staff involved
and that, as a result, inconsistencies and
differences in practice remained. Little mention
was made of the staff meetings held or of specific
initiatives such as the drawing up and
distribution of the Note of Guidance to staff.
Two unfortunate effects were believed to have
resulted from what was perceived to have been the
failure of the consultation process: first, the
setting up of an initial programme that had made
more demands on staff than on trainees, and
secondly poor staff commitment to the new regime.

4.25 Although critical of the new regime in
operation, and the way it had been introduced, the
majority (31) of staff favoured stricter and more
demanding standards in detention centres or called
for more effective staff authority. Twenty called
for renewed emphasis on work, training and a
return of incentive, and 13 argued for a return,
substantially, to the old regime. When New Hall
had been chosen to operate the new regime many had
taken this as a compliment and as recognition that
their existing standards and their existing regime
met with approval. A few had had reservations.
They had feared an increase in violence, self-
injuries or even suicides and they had been
concerned for their own professional safety. For
the majority the new regime had come nowhere near
to living up to their expectations (good or bad)
although there were some who felt that now things
had begun to settle down at last (towards the end
of 1980), the new regime would prove both workable
and effective. Among those who were initially
unenthusiastic about the whole concept of a
deterrent regime there was relief that their fears
had proved unfounded.

4.26 As to improving on the new regime, fewer interruptions to the working day and a greater emphasis on discipline were considered preferable to any increase in activity. By far the most frequently called for change was towards stricter, more austere and disciplined conditions with few 'extras' (education, probation interviews, and visits) to interrupt the basic working day. The interviews provoked a fair range of proposals about dealing with young offenders, the significant point being that only one member of staff said he would keep the new regime more or less as it was at the time, whereas well over half favoured a regime that they considered would be yet more demanding.

At Send

4.27 The staff interviewed at Send covered a range of grades similar to those at New Hall; 24 discipline staff were interviewed (another three refused), together with five full-time teachers, two probation officers and the chaplain. The replies of the discipline staff are presented first.

4.28 Whilst the response of many of the discipline officers at Send was very similar in many respects to those at New Hall, there were some important differences. Thus although the majority of Send officers (18) criticised the implementation of the new regime on much the same grounds as the New Hall officers (carried out too quickly and without sufficient consideration for 'grass-roots' opinion), more of the Send officers saw the regime as a significant improvement over the old system (13 held this view as against 11 who considered the changes merely superficial alterations to the existing regime).

4.29 As at New Hall, most officers (22) had been
enthusiastic about the prospect when the intention
to introduce a new regime was first announced, but
only nine were now satisfied that the regime in
operation matched up to their initial
expectations: ten had expected something tougher
and five maintained that they had always regarded
the plan as a political gesture.

4.30 None of the officers said they handled
trainees differently, reflecting, in a more
decisive way, the response of the New Hall staff.

4.31 There were similar anxieties about conflict
between staff and similar divisions between those
who had Forces experience of drill and those too
young to have known National Service. Twelve
thought Send currently to be a less pleasant place
in which to work whereas eight considered it had
improved, and 13 thought their jobs had become
more difficult.

4.32 Nevertheless a greater proportion of the
officers at Send liked the new system (10 out of
the 24 interviewed). Fifteen officers felt that
the new regime was beneficial in that the trainees
appeared to find it hard and that was judged to be
a good thing. However, seven qualified this view
by stressing that they considered it was only the
first few days that were really hard, and after
that, the trainees settled into the routine and
the effect was lost. Only one thought the regime
detrimental. Sixteen of the 24 officers
interviewed said that the new routine was more
interesting for trainees; it made the days pass
quickly for them and the fast pace and constant
change of activity made it easier for them to 'do
their best'. Ten felt that the centre was running
better as a result. It is probably this sense of
the centre running smoothly that most
characterised the difference between Send and New

134

Hall officers. At Send the detail (the assignment of officers to posts) had become much more continuous than it had been before the pilot project. As a consequence officers who had formerly not known which dormitory group or work party they were assigned to supervise until they arrived on duty preferred the new regime where there was much more continuity in the tasks officers were given to do. This appeared not only to enhance job satisfaction in the sense that officers now got to know the trainees as individuals but also (probably for the same reasons) to increase their feelings of being in control. So whilst Send officers often complained about drill (how it interfered with work) and about receiving the 'wrong sort of inmate' (ie. one that was too criminally sophisticated to be much deterred) and that the regime was over-programmed (the schedule was too tight causing logistic problems such as moving inmates from place to place in the time available) there was a sense of achievement too.

4.33 Nine officers stated that the boys were better behaved under the new system, 11 noticed no change and four said that the trainees were more difficult now. This is particularly interesting in view of the findings reported elsewhere that there was an increase in disciplinary reports after the change in regime and supports the contention that this increase reflected a difference in how officers handled misbehaviour rather than a change in the behaviour itself.

4.34 Of the eight specialists interviewed most (7) felt that the changes would have no effect on the trainees and almost as many (6) subscribed to the view that the change in regime was merely a political gesture rather than a true penal experiment.

4.35 As Send is a junior detention centre, it has a larger education element than at New Hall. At the time roughly two thirds of the trainees were below school leaving age and thus required full-time education. In order to accommodate the extra PE within the new regime the education period had been reduced. Seven of the specialist staff who were surveyed said that this was the most important change in the regime and a retrograde step. In fact, six of them took the view that the other changes (ie. drill, the change into uniform, extra PE etc) were merely cosmetic. Many of the negative views appeared to flow from this. The full-time education staff, all of whom were interviewed, felt that their task had become more difficult, that Send was a less pleasant place to work in, and that they would rather work under the old system.

4.36 Their view of the new regime was that it reduced the trainees' involvement in education and their choice of evening classes, but that the greater movement about the centre meant that the trainees spent less time at unpleasant tasks. Only one said that in his view the regime was harder, whereas five thought that it was easier. Overall, the specialists were doubtful that the new regime would have a deterrent effect.

The second staff survey

4.37 The purpose of the second survey was to obtain some measure of staff opinion about the new regime in operation once it had had time to settle down and was thus free from contamination by unrest or the upsetting consequence of recent change.

4.38 For this reason it was decided to focus primarily on elements central to the new regime and the emphasis put on them in day-to-day running. In particular it was considered important to discover whether staff saw the regime as it operated to be in agreement with the 'blueprint' set down in the Note of Guidance.

4.39 A more structured approach was adopted than in the first survey. First, each interview was preceded by a card-sort. The cards employed at Send and New Hall were almost identical - 44 items at Send and 46 at New Hall (see Note 4.1). Briefly, each card presented the subject with a straightforward choice between two more or less opposing statements about the regime, each statement being built around key words identified within the text of the Note of Guidance.

4.40 Secondly, a priori scales were employed within the interview to rate responses to each question and although, in addition, a comprehensive note was made of the main features of each reply, detailed transcriptions were not produced. Inevitably this resulted in the interviews being more forced and less conversational than had been the case in the first survey and allowed subjects much less scope to explain their views fully. At Send 40 members of staff were invited to take part: one declined and one failed to complete the interview due to scheduling difficulties. At New Hall 44 members of staff were invited: four declined saying they doubted whether notice would be taken of the 'grass roots'. Once again the intention was to include as many of those in daily contact with trainees as possible.

4.41 The interview schedule employed in the second survey was closely tied to the Note of Guidance to Staff, as far as possible actual phrases from the Note being used in formulating the questions asked.

4.42 The interview covered five main areas:-

i.   **The main elements in the new regime.**
     This section focussed on those parts of
     the regime in which the Note of Guidance
     required change or particular emphasis:
     drill and marching; fitness training and
     physical education; hard physical work;
     cleanliness and tidiness; discipline and
     respect for other people; the rigour and
     demands of the regime.

ii. **The effect on the centre.**
     In this section staff were asked for
     their comments on the running of the
     detention centre and on the consequences
     of the new regime for staff.

iii. **The effect on the trainees.**
     In this part of the interview staff were
     asked if they thought the new regime
     would deter trainees from committing
     further offences, whether they
     considered any aspects of the regime to
     have particularly deterring effects, or
     to be found particularly difficult by
     trainees, and whether they thought that
     the trainees found the regime as a whole
     hard or easy, interesting or boring.

iv. **The officers' behaviour under the new
     regime.**
     Staff opinion was sought on the level of
     supervision of trainees, the effect of
     the change on staff-trainee
     relationships, and on their perception
     of the trainees' response to the demands
     made on them by staff.

v.　**Suggestions for change.**
　　Finally the staff were asked two open-
　　ended questions on ways in which they
　　believed the regime could be improved
　　and the changes they would introduce had
　　they the opportunity.

4.43 Each participant was asked three questions
about each of the elements of the regime listed in
section i. above:-

　　i.　how much emphasis was placed on that
　　　　element under the new regime;

　　ii.　whether that represented an increase or
　　　　a decrease in emphasis over the previous
　　　　regime;

　　iii. whether, in the subject's opinion, the
　　　　current level of emphasis was about
　　　　right or should be changed.

4.44 Replies to the first type of question ought
to provide some evidence on the extent to which
staff saw the regime in operation as measuring up
to the guidelines. Replies to the second type
ought to provide information on their view of the
size and direction of the changes that had
actually taken place. Finally replies to the
third type ought to provide some insights into
their own assessments of the advantages and
disadvantages in the change of regime. Questions
in the remaining sections were similar although
the actual form varied slightly to suit the
specific topic. In particular attention was paid
to any contrast between the new regime and its
predecessor.

4.45 In the event, responses to the card-sort
statements closely agreed with replies given in

interview although they did provide some
additional information, for instance, on the
staff's perceptions about the physical hardness of
the work on the various parties. With this
exception, therefore, the result of the card-sort
will not be discussed separately and the reader is
referred to Note 4.1 at the end of this chapter
where the statements appearing on each card,
together with the number of staff at Send and New
Hall who endorsed each, are presented. What is
worthy of note, however, is the similarity in the
proportions of staff in each establishment
endorsing particular views. There were very few
examples indeed of the staff of Send taking one
view and those of New Hall taking the other.

At New Hall

4.46 Most were agreed (37) that a lot of emphasis
was placed on drill and all but one of those with
experience of the previous regime that this
represented a considerable increase. Twenty five
out of the 40 members of staff interviewed
believed that the emphasis on drill was too great
although criticism of drill was by no means always
associated with a belief that it should be
abandoned completely.

4.47 The majority (34) thought that considerable
emphasis was placed on parades and inspections
although there was disagreement over whether there
had been any real increase, 16 saying there had
been, 13 claiming little or no change, and five
actually claiming a reduction. Where the emphasis
was thought to have changed in particular was in
relation to parades: inspections were seen as
having always been a central feature of life at
New Hall. Evidently most of those interviewed
thought parades and inspections important. Almost
half believed the current level to be correct and
a further 15 thought yet more emphasis should be

placed on this particular feature of the regime, not by increasing their frequency but by demanding more stringent standards and imposing more effective sanctions should those standards not be reached. Most staff (34) thought that considerable emphasis was placed on cleanliness and tidiness but that there had been little change from the days of the old regime (23). The majority (26) were satisfied with the current high standards but some (14) argued that one could never have too much cleanliness: it was an essential requirement whenever large numbers of people lived closely together. Although standards of personal hygiene were thought by most to be little changed a few staff expressed the opinion that the increased traffic through the dormitories and main corridor resulting from the new timetable, together with reduced time available at weekends for thorough cleaning, meant that these areas were not now as clean and tidy as before. Opinion differed somewhat over whether discipline and respect for others were prominent under the new regime, production staff[2] tending to be more critical than discipline staff, most of whom considered the standards to be good. There was, however, agreement that the new regime had brought no improvement in this respect: 20 reckoned there had been no change and the other 14 with experience of both regimes thought there had been a reduction in emphasis.

4.48 Eight of those interviewed considered that quite a lot of emphasis still was placed on hard physical work, whereas 20 claimed that it now

---

[2] Those staff responsible for production or for the provision of a service and thus subject to time constraints: loomshop instructor, farm and gardens staff, kitchen staff, works staff, storeman.

received relatively little emphasis. Thirty of
the 34 having experience of both regimes
considered that the emphasis on hard physical work
had been reduced and no one thought it had
increased. Perhaps it was not surprising,
therefore, that the majority of staff (34)
favoured reversing this perceived reduction.

4.49 Of the 10 work areas at New Hall mentioned in
the card-sort only four were regarded by the
majority of staff as being physically hard. The
loomshop was most widely regarded as providing
physically hard work, but even here a number
qualified their response by saying that this
depended on the production target: when there was
a heavy demand for bed-rugs the loomshop could
provide physically demanding work that was also
unremitting. Working on the farm party, in the
dairy, and chopping and sawing logs were also seen
by the majority as hard but, once again, subject
to provisos. The hardness of the farm party
depended upon season, weather and task. The dairy
party was noted more for the long hours, the pace
and the responsibility rather than because it was
heavy work. Most pointed out that chopping and
sawing logs rarely took place.

4.50 By contrast, the work of the orderlies,
working for the works department, and cleaning the
centre were regarded by most as requiring
relatively little effort normally.

4.51 Views about the rigour and demandingness of
the regime as a whole also differed. Three
quarters of the discipline staff considered the
new regime demanding whereas only three out of 13
production staff regarded it so. However, over
half of those with experience of both regimes
considered the new one to be less rigorous and
demanding (19 out of 34) whereas only five thought
it more so. The majority (35 out of the 40

questioned) expressed a preference for an increase in rigour although there were different opinions about what this would entail.

4.52 The predominant view across all groups of staff was that the centre was once again running well. Despite this only one staff member considered that the introduction of the new regime had brought any improvement whereas almost all noted at least one area which they thought had deteriorated. Most of the staff liked working at New Hall but for many this was despite the change in the regime. Well over half felt that their jobs had become harder and this view tended to be expressed more strongly by production staff because of the problems of organising the work within shorter periods. Nearly three quarters of the staff felt that there was conflict at New Hall though most felt that this took place only at a personal level and that, despite any conflict, most staff 'pulled together' most of the time. By and large the new regime was not seen as the cause of this conflict though some felt that it tended to exacerbate existing problems between staff.

4.53 Five members of the staff interviewed felt that the regime was an effective deterrent. The balance of opinion was that the current regime was less deterrent than its predecessor although a substantial proportion (16 out of the 34 holding this view) maintained that there was little difference. Opinions varied as to the reason for the presumed lack of deterrent effect. Some doubted the long term effectiveness of any deterrent approach, others argued that the trainees received were already so steeped in crime or accustomed to prison routines (through long periods on remand) that they could not be deterred. When discussing the deterrent value of particular parts of the regime the majority view was again that none was particularly successful.

Some felt, however, that the initial stage of the
sentence was hardest for the trainees and one or
two argued that the standards of behaviour and
performance required at New Hall benefitted the
trainees as people, whether or not they had any
effect upon the likelihood of reoffending.

4.54 Most staff claimed that after the first week
or two trainees generally found the regime
comparatively easy, and just over half felt that
the new regime was easier than the previous one
(only three considered it harder). The main
reason given for this view was that the move from
work to drill and PE had increased the variety
within the daily programme. They considered it to
be a busy routine rather than one which trainees
found hard.

4.55 Supervision of trainees was thought to be
close though only a fifth went so far as to say
that trainees were very closely supervised. There
was a division in staff view over whether the
level of supervision had changed. Some staff
pointed out that, since there were now activities
such as drill in which close supervision is an
integral part of the activity, supervision was by
definition closer. On the other hand, those staff
who maintained that there had been some
deterioration in this aspect of the regime argued
that the more frequent changeover in activities
provided an increased opportunity to 'skive'.

4.56 Throughout the introduction of the new
regime it had been the intention to safeguard
what were believed to be reasonably good
relationships between staff and trainees. The
consensus from the interviews was that a
satisfactory balance had been maintained between
good relationships and 'keeping the trainees at
it'. The only dissent was from works staff who

felt that they had less opportunity now to get to know the trainees well. The trainees' response to staff was thought largely unchanged and to have remained good.

4.57 When asked to make suggestions as to how the regime could be changed, most staff responses centred round the desire to return to a more straightforward timetable in which uninterrupted work was the main daytime activity. Substantial minorities spoke of their desire to see improvements in the approach of, and standards required by, local staff (8), wished for the return of incentives which they considered had been eroded (7), or wanted to increase the officer's on-the-spot control (5).

At Send

4.58 There was little difference between officers and civilians in most of their views about the main elements within the regime. Thus the majority of staff believed that drill (30), cleanliness and tidiness (30) were at least 'sufficiently' emphasised within the new regime. The one activity stressed in the Note of Guidance which many of the staff felt received too little emphasis was physically hard work, nearly 50% of those expressing an opinion (18 out of 37) taking this view.

4.59 When asked to comment on the changes in the regime the response was similar. Three quarters of those interviewed considered that there had been an increase in emphasis on drill and roughly half thought that the emphasis on fitness training and PE had increased. There was broad agreement that standards of cleanliness and tidiness, and discipline and respect for others had been maintained, although some pointed out that Send always had had high standards in these areas:

there had been little scope for improvement.
Discipline officers and civilian specialists
differed somewhat in their view of how emphasis on
hard physical work had changed within the regime.
Whereas almost all of the civilians took the view
that the emphasis had not reduced (opinion was
evenly split over whether or not it had
increased), over half of the discipline staff
believed that less emphasis was now placed on this
aspect of the regime. However, many of those
reporting a reduction suggested that, although the
work was often not physically demanding, this was
a result of fluctuating demands imposed by
circumstances beyond their control, such as the
weather affecting work in the market gardens.
Obviously work out of doors is harder and
physically more arduous in winter than in summer
and there is not much that can be done about that.
Similarly, when numbers in the detention centre
fall, work for the few becomes more demanding than
when there is an excess of labour.

4.60 The card-sort revealed that, at Send, staff
opinion was more evenly split than at New Hall
over whether the work on the various parties was
physically hard. Kitchen work, working in the
laundry and on the (ornamental) garden party were
regarded by a narrow majority as being physically
hard and only the work of the orderlies was
regarded by most to require little physical
effort.

4.61 Regarding all of those areas within which the
Note of Guidance had required increased emphasis
there was an almost equal division between those
who felt that the centre was operating 'about
right' and others who felt that more could be done
to increase the rigour of the experience. The
exception here was drill where about one quarter
believed that the emphasis could be reduced.
Overwhelmingly the staff felt that Send was well

organised although a substantial minority (9 out
of 26) were dissatisfied with the change that had
been made. The thing most often praised by those
who liked the new regime was the increased
continuity. Some staff now found themselves
assigned to the same duties for a considerable
period, for example officers were now attached to
the same dormitory and could more easily get to
know those in their charge. It was generally for
those sorts of reasons that 10 staff said their
job was now easier than three years ago.

4.62 Most staff liked the new system, mainly
because they had more of a sense of control.
Nevertheless, many complained of conflict between
groups of staff: 14 said that this was serious
conflict and 19 thought that the conflict was
minor, whereas three chose to emphasise that staff
were working together well. The reasons put
forward for this conflict were various. Some of
those who thought that it was not serious
suggested that the smallness of the institution
created a situation where minor details became
exaggerated. Others suggested that it was a
question of personalities where a small group of
the officers were 'out of step' with the aims and
methods of the new regime and that this created
antagonism. Of those who suggested that the
conflict was more serious some indicated that the
problem lay in the gap between senior and junior
staff and between those who knew how to implement
what could be seen as a military system because
they came from a service background and those who
had no such experience.

4.63 Nearly all of those interviewed (36) rated
their relationship with the trainees as good or
very good and 17 considered that there had been no
change in this respect. 'Firm but fair' were the
adjectives most often used by staff to
characterise their approach to the trainees.

Occasionally a member of staff would assert that there was really little opportunity to develop a relationship with the trainees since the tempo of the regime and the shortness of the sentence prevented more than a superficial interaction between staff and boys, but such reservations were rare. The response from the trainees to this firm but fair handling was not generally rated as less than good (only two suggested they received a poor response from trainees).

4.64 Eight of those interviewed felt that the response had improved under the new system, and 17 thought it unchanged. When it came to judging the effect of the new regime only three members of the staff thought that the regime really would deter trainees from further offending. Although nearly half (16) felt that the experience had some deterrent value, 18 doubted the deterrent effect of the regime. Most felt that the changes to the regime had not affected this greatly (19), although a fifth of those with experience of both regimes (5) considered that the likely deterrent effects had increased.

4.65 Staff generally expressed the view that the trainees found the regime easy (23), although most qualified this by saying that the induction procedure was experienced as hard. As a result many welcomed the shorter detention sentence proposed in the then Criminal Justice Bill, believing that thereby trainees would be released back into the community before the initial impact had worn off.

4.66 Many, officers particularly, were surprised by the question of whether trainees found the regime interesting or not. Often the reply was that it was not meant to be interesting to trainees and many of them were reluctant to view the detention centre experience in these terms.

In discussion about this they were agreed that under the new regime there were more changes in activity (parades, drill, work, education) during the day and that as a consequence the trainees would not have had time to be bored, but they did not like to apply the adjective 'interesting', almost as if such a word would imply softness inappropriate to a tougher regime.

4.67 None of those interviewed felt that the trainees in general behaved badly at Send, and 19 out of the 21 expressing a definite view expressed the opinion that trainees were better behaved under the new system. However, the major reason for this rating appeared to be the recent change in catchment area [3]. As a consequence of this change fewer inner city boys were now received (and virtually no black trainees). The effect had been that the street-smart inner city youngster who had proved such a handful to staff, now rarely appeared. The passing of this group was noted with regret by some of the staff for, it was said, a degree of job interest had departed too.

4.68 There was agreement that trainees were closely supervised, the only division being between those who felt that this amounted to 'very close scrutiny' and those who admitted to it being merely 'close'. Over a quarter felt that the level of supervision had improved. Two areas were often mentioned as not tightly supervised: the orderlies (where it was admitted that this did not matter greatly, since these were carefully selected trainees) and the market gardens and amenities parties, where the nature of the work meant that trainees often worked with over-view by a patrolling officer.

---

[3] This change in catchment area occurred in July 1981. (It did not affect New Hall.)

4.69 With regard to the level of emphasis on PE and fitness training, all but one of those who had joined since the introduction of the new regime judged it to be about right. However amongst those with a longer experience of Send opinion was more diverse: four considered that less emphasis should be given to PE, 13 accepted that the current level was about right, and nine argued for an increase in emphasis.

DISCUSSION

4.70 The replies from staff were detailed and not only contained expressions of opinion but also descriptions of events brought to mind as evidence for the assertions made.

4.71 The varying nature of the opinions and the sometimes conflicting views presented can only add to the difficulty of interpreting and understanding the findings. It is necessary to recognise that basically similar views of a particular complex event can give rise to seemingly conflicting answers purely as a result of the respondents choosing to focus on one aspect of the event rather than another. Consider, for example, what the first survey revealed about staff reactions at New Hall when the intention to introduce a new regime in detention centres was first announced. In their replies some showed themselves to have been enthusiastic at the prospect of a more disciplined regime whereas others felt apprehensive about the risks that would be involved. But it was clear that there were few who in reality were not aware of those risks and who were not, to varying degrees, worried about them, and it was only a small minority who did not believe that the detention centres would benefit from being tightened up in one respect or another. Thus the significance of

some of the findings lies not so much in the
relative proportions of staff taking each line in
the course of the interviews as in the fact that
these two aspects of the staff response to the
announcements co-existed, and in the effect that
these apparently conflicting considerations
subsequently had on the way the new regime was put
into effect.

4.72 The images of the regimes generated in the
media during the period which followed the
announcement accorded with many of the officers'
beliefs about the proper management of
delinquents. However, the extent of the public
interest brought a realisation that running a
genuinely tougher regime would bring added risks,
pressures and responsibilities on themselves.
Some were reluctant to be cast in a more negative
light; they gained satisfaction from the
opportunities their work gave them to help and to
train. Many were reluctant to accept changes in
their role which might be seen as confirming what
they saw as their own very negative image in the
eyes of the public at large. By April when the
new regime was brought into use, much of the
initial enthusiasm for a toughening up of
conditions had been replaced by opposition towards
the new regime which most staff now saw as being
imposed on them. Their replies revealed some of
the factors which had contributed to that change.
The consultation process which they felt had been
compressed due to the urgency of the promised
implementation had left them feeling that local
staff opinion and experience had not been taken
into account. Also there were issues relating,
for example, to drill instruction, more parochial
concerns such as the loss of the skilled
labourer's course at New Hall, and staff views
that the maximum population at Send should be
reduced before the implementation. So the first
staff survey provided some information about the

issues surrounding the introduction of the new
regime, the staff view of its initial operation,
and the strength of feeling that accompanied its
implementation.

4.73 The new regime had been in operation for two
years by the time the second survey was conducted
and the questions focussed on the regime as it was
operating rather than on the process of change.
The replies were rather more restrained.
Nevertheless, there was still quite a lot of
criticism of the new regime and many of the
opinions given on this second occasion echoed
those expressed so forcefully in the course of the
first survey.

4.74 Staff generally saw drill, PE, parades and
inspections, and standards of cleanliness and
tidiness as receiving a high level of emphasis
within the new regime although it was only in
relation to PE and drill that there was thought to
have been an appreciable increase. Inspections
and parades had always been central to the regime
day and standards of cleanliness and tidiness were
judged always to have been good. There is
remarkable concordance between the two centres in
these views.

4.75 By and large the staff of the two centres did
not point to any marked way in which their own
input had changed. The introduction of drill was
seen by most staff to have increased the element
of close supervision within the regime and there
was evidence that they sought and received high
standards on the parade ground. But in most other
respects the majority of staff reported the
maintenance of high standards (at inspections, in
cleanliness and tidiness, and in discipline and
respect of others) rather than any further
tightening up of what was required. Most felt
that their relations with trainees had not changed

appreciably and that 'firm but fair' was still the
order of the day.

4.76 The surveys revealed quite a lot of
information about the trainees' response to the
new regime and some of the elements within it, as
perceived by staff. As will already be clear,
they commented favourably on the trainees'
behaviour and general response, and on the effort
most showed, on the parade square, for example.
But many observed that trainees were soon able to
adapt to the demands made of them. Thus Send
staff commented that most trainees found the
regime easy, but only once the induction period
was over, and staff at New Hall reported that
trainees found drill and PE hard, but only at
first. Regimentation, having to take orders, and
the exacting standards of kit preparation and
inspections were seen as elements within the
regime which most trainees found fairly demanding
throughout the sentence.

4.77 Criticism of the new regime at New Hall
focussed largely on what staff saw as the reduced
emphasis on work. Most staff would have preferred
a return towards a more simple daily programme,
one uninterrupted by additional PE sessions and
shortened only at the beginning of the sentence by
drill training. At Send drill and extra PE time
were not so severely criticised by the discipline
staff (partly since the space allocated to extra
PE came from education time, an activity of low
priority in many of the discipline staff's view).
Teachers at Send, on the other hand, were unhappy
at the reduction of education entailed by the new
timetable.

4.78 Comparatively little of the trainees' work
was widely regarded by the staff of either centre
as being consistently physically hard but at New
Hall in particular there was the further complaint

that the introduction of drill and PE periods had
reduced total working time and had shortened some
of the work periods. A number of officers
commented that the supervision of some work
parties had become somewhat easier, that it was
easier to 'keep the lads at it' because the
trainees were no longer on any particular job long
enough to get bored with it. On the other hand,
instructors and craftsmen complained that they no
longer had their (selected) trainees for long
enough to get them really interested in their
work, and that controlling trainees was harder as
the same amount of work needed to be done in a
shorter time, and trainees therefore were required
to work harder.

4.79 But in most respects such divisions between
staff as there were did not coincide with
vocational or grade boundaries. Cluster analyses
(see Note 4.2) carried out on responses to the
card-sort revealed fairly distinct groupings of
staff. In each establishment groups of moderate
opinion, satisfied with standards and response but
doubtful of the deterrent effect of the regime and
of the long term benefit to trainees, groups
highly critical of almost every element in the new
regime, and groups either accepting or doubting
the place of education in such a regime, were
found. To a degree these differences in view
continued to generate minor tensions among staff
and to accentuate some of the conflicts which were
already there. But since, for most, they focussed
around how things should be rather than how they
were, their effect on day to day operations was
limited.

4.80 In as far as it is possible to summarise the
staff view which emerged of the regime as a whole
it was that the new regime in operation did
measure up in most respects to the requirements
set down in the guidelines but that, in practice,

154

it did not constitute a tougher, more demanding, or more deterrent regime. Their appraisal of the regime appears to have been based largely on their observation that most trainees enjoy PE and, to a lesser degree, prefer drill to many of the other activities and on the commonsense reasoning that deterrent effect will not be boosted by increasing the amount of time given over to preferred activities. Most were convinced that trainees came to find the present regime easy but that the busy programme made staff's lives harder.

4.81 In spite of these criticisms the majority of staff in both centres now felt that the regimes were once again running more smoothly, that trainees were remarkably well behaved and responsive and that staff/inmate relationships were good.

4.82 During these long interviews one could not help being struck by the high standards that staff set themselves. The criticisms the staff levelled at their performance (albeit corporate performance) stemmed perhaps from their high expectations of what they should achieve. Much of what they had understood would happen was influenced by the stark pictures presented in the newspapers and on television in the period before the Note of Guidance became available. The sensational images of the kind of regime that would be implemented were not realised by the changes introduced.

Note 4.1 Responses to the card sort[4]

A. Deterrence – the deterrent qualities of the regime

	Question	New Hall	Send
1.	a. This regime effectively deters trainees from committing further offences.	6	7
	b. This regime is not much of a deterrent.	34	31
	Undecided	–	–
3.	a. Most of the trainees here find the regime hard.	9	11
	b. Most of the trainees find the regime here easy.	31	27
	Undecided	–	–
9.	a. This regime is a tough one.	2	8
	b. The regime here is not really tough.	38	30
	. Undecided	–	–
17.	a. The trainees find this regime a demanding one.	23	20
	b. Few demands are made of the trainees here.	17	18
	Undecided	–	–

---

[4] Steps were taken to counter effects which might be produced by the order in which the options for each question were put. This involved alternating use in both centres of a second pack in which the order of the options was reversed.

		Question	New Hall	Send
25.	a.	This regime is more rigorous and demanding than the previous regime.	7	9
	b.	This regime is not more rigorous and demanding than the previous one.	33	22
		Undecided	-	7

B. Standards – the standards set in the regime

		Question	New Hall	Send
5.	a.	The trainees have to prepare very thoroughly for the inspections here.	27	35
	b.	Trainees here are a little slapdash in their preparation for inspections.	13	2
		Undecided	-	1
19.	a.	Discipline is an important part of this regime.	35	36
	b.	Discipline is not an important part of this regime.	5	2
		Undecided	-	-
24.	a.	The daily drill sessions are conducted in a smart manner.	38	28
	b.	The daily drill sessions are often sloppy.	2	10
		Undecided	-	-
26.	a.	The inspections held in this institution are very thorough.	30	31
	b.	Little attention is paid to detail in the inspections here.	10	6
		Undecided	7	1

	Question	New Hall	Send
27.	a. Tidiness is something that is stressed in the regime.	33	29
	b. Not enough emphasis is placed on tidiness here.	7	9
	Undecided	-	-
33.	a. In this regime the proper emphasis is placed on discipline.	19	24
	b. This regime lacks the proper emphasis on discipline.	21	14
	Undecided	-	-

C. Supervision – the level of supervision

	Question	New Hall	Send
18.	a. Trainees are closely supervised whilst doing PE.	37	36
	b. Sometimes trainees on PE are not closely supervised.	3	1
	Undecided	-	1
42.	a. Trainees are closely supervised whilst on work parties.	19	19
	b. Sometimes trainees on work parties are not closely supervised.	21	19
	Undecided	-	-
44.	a. Trainees are closely supervised during drill training.	38	34
	b. Sometimes trainees are not closely supervised during drill training.	2	4
	Undecided	-	-

D. Response – the trainees' response to standards

	Question	New Hall	Send
8.	a. The level of discipline is good during drill.	40	32
	b. Trainees often misbehave during drill.	0	6
	Undecided	-	-

		Question	New Hall	Send
13.	a.	The parades here always reach very much the same standard.	30	24
	b.	The standard achieved on parade varies a lot from day to day.	10	13
		Undecided	-	1
21.	a.	The trainees soon learn to parade smartly.	35	27
	b.	Trainees have great difficulty in learning to parade smartly.	5	11
		Undecided	-	-
32.	a.	The Sunday* parades are almost always smart.	36	31
	b.	The parades on Sunday* are occasionally sloppy.	4	6
		Undecided (*Saturday at Send)	-	1
41.	a.	The trainees take a pride in their appearance during drill sessions.	36	28
	b.	During the drill periods the trainees are slovenly in their bearing.	4	10
		Undecided	-	-

E.   Work - the hardness of the work

		Question	New Hall	Send
4.	a.	Working in the compound* is physically hard for the trainees.	15	12
	b.	Not much physical effort is required from the trainees who work in the compound*.	25	26
		Undecided (*market garden at Send) -		-

			Question	New Hall	Send
6.	a.		Working for the works department is physically hard for the trainees.	7	15
	b.		Not much physical effort is required from the trainees who work for the works department.	33	23
			Undecided	-	1
12.	a.		Working in the kitchen is physically hard for the trainees.	18	23
	b.		Not much physical effort is required from the trainees who work in the kitchen.	22	15
			Undecided	-	-
14.	a.		Chopping and sawing wood is physically hard for trainees.	25	-
	b.		Not much physical effort is required from the trainees when they have to chop and saw wood.	15	-
			Undecided (Not administered at Send) -		-
20.	a.		Working at cleaning the centre is physically hard for the trainees.	9	17
	b.		Not much physical effort is required from the trainees who work cleaning the centre.	31	21
			Undecided	-	-
28.	a.		Working as an orderly in the centre is physically hard for the trainees.	3	7
	b.		Not much physical effort is required from the trainees who work as orderlies in the centre.	37	31
			Undecided		
34.	a.		Working in the dairy is physically hard for the trainees.	27	-
	b.		Not much physical effort is required from the trainees who work in the dairy.	13	-
			Undecided (Not applicable to Send) -		-

Question	New Hall	Send

34. a. Working in the laundry is physically hard for the trainees. — 21
     b. Not much physical effort is required from the trainees who work in the laundry. — 16
     Undecided — 1
     (Not applicable to New Hall)

39. a. Working on the gardens party is physically hard for the trainees (ornamental gardens). 14 21
     b. Not much physical effort is required from the trainees who work on the gardens party (ornamental gardens). 26 17
     Undecided — —

45. a. Working on the farm party is physically hard for the trainees. 30 —
     b. Not much physical effort is required from the trainees who work on the farm party. 10 —
     Undecided (Not applicable to Send) — —

46. a. Working in the loomshop is physically hard for the trainees. 33 —
     b. Not much physical effort is required from the trainees who work in the loomshop. 7 —
     Undecided (Not applicable to Send) — —

F. Benefit – general or lasting effects on trainees

Question	New Hall	Send

2. a. PE makes the trainees much fitter. 38 37
    b. Trainees' physical fitness is not much improved by the PE. 2 1
    Undecided — —

	Question	New Hall	Send
10.	a. The physical skills the trainees acquire in PE classes will benefit them on their release.	9	11
	b. Any benefit the trainees gain through PE is soon lost after release.	31	27
	Undecided	–	–
11.	a. Most of the activities the trainees engage in here will benefit them later.	9	13
	b. Few of the activities the trainees engage in here will be of benefit to them later.	31	25
	Undecided	–	–
16.	a. Drill teaches the trainees self-discipline.	27	29
	b. The experience of drill has little effect on the trainees' self-discipline.	13	9
	Undecided	–	–
23.	a. The education trainees receive in detention centre will benefit them after release.	18	17
	b. Any benefit gained from education classes is lost after the trainees are released.	22	21
	Undecided	–	–
35.	a. The teamwork the trainees learn during drill will benefit them later.	14	13
	b. The teamwork the trainees learn on parade has little effect after they are released.	26	25
	Undecided	–	–

	Question	New Hall	Send
36.	a. Having to do work that is physically hard will benefit the trainees after release.	15	22
	b. Any benefit gained through working physically hard is soon lost after the trainees are released.	25	16
	Undecided	-	-
38.	a. The effect of being drilled is that trainees learn to move smartly even when not on the parade ground.	23	29
	b. Drill training has little effect on trainees' bearing when not on the parade ground.	17	9
	Undecided	-	-
43.	a. The trainees gain little except physical fitness from PE.	16	14
	b. Physical education is generally good for the trainees.	24	24
	Undecided	-	-

G   Education - its place in the pilot project

	Question	New Hall	Send
7.	a. In the education department the trainees work hard.	9	21
	b. Trainees take it easy during the education classes.	31	17
	Undecided	-	-
15.	a. The education classes are a useful part of the regime here.	18	19
	b. Education classes have little useful function in the detention centre.	22	19
	Undecided	-	-

	Question	New Hall	Send
31.	a. The trainees are well behaved in the education classes.	24	23
	b. The trainees misbehave in the education classes.	16	15
	Undecided	-	-
40.	a. Discipline in the education classes is as strict as in the rest of the institution.	15	17
	b. Discipline in the education classes is less strict than in the rest of the institution.	25	21
	Undecided	-	-

Uncategorised – not easily fitting any scales

	Question	New Hall	Send
22.	a. Trainees spend longer at work under the new regime.	0	6
	b. Under the new regime trainees do not spend as much time at work.	40	28
	Undecided	-	4
29.	a. The best results are obtained by being strict with the trainees when teaching them drill.	20	17
	b. When teaching drill the best results are obtained by getting the trainees' enthusiasm for the parade.	20	21
	Undecided	-	-
30.	a. Physically hard work is an important part of the regime here.	30	36
	b. Hard physical work has little value in the detention centre's regime.	10	2
	Undecided		

Question	New Hall	Send
37. a. Physical education is an important part of this regime.	32	34
b. Physical education serves little useful function in this regime.	8	4
Undecided	-	-

Note 4.2 Cluster analysis of card-sort data

4.83 In order to investigate the degree to which
groupings of opinion existed among the staff of
the two centres, the card-sort data were subject
to further statistical investigation in the form
of a cluster analysis. Cluster analysis is a
mathematical technique which may be used to group
entities (in this case members of the staff of the
two centres) on the basis of similarities in data
relating to them (in this case scale-scores based
on their responses to the card-sort statements).
The clustering technique employed here (Ward's
method) begins by grouping together the two
subjects most similar to one another and proceeds
step-by-step to add other subjects on the basis of
their similarity to clusters already formed (or
their greater similarity to another subject, thus
beginning another cluster). Ultimately this
technique coalesces all of the clusters into one
containing all of the subjects and it is necessary
to halt the procedure several steps short of this
at a point at which most of the variation within
the data remains and yet the number of clusters
formed is manageably small. (For a detailed
account of the methodology see Everitt 1974.) The
data from Send and New Hall were analysed
separately. In each case four reasonably distinct
clusters were identified.

At New Hall

Cluster I (n=15)

4.84 Most members of this the largest group rated the standards, level of supervision and response of the trainees highly and held moderate views about the place of education in the detention centre. In contrast they were very doubtful of the deterrent value of the regime, were relatively unimpressed by the hardness of the work and held only moderate views about the benefit trainees might derive. Essentially they were a moderate group, reasonably satisfied with the balance in the centre but unimpressed by attempts to toughen the regime and to deter.

Cluster II (n=19)

4.85 This was the only group that came near to regarding the current regime as being tough. By and large they appeared content with the standards required of trainees, the level of supervision, and with the response of trainees and the benefit they were presumed to derive. However, it was their favourable view of the education in the centre which most distinguished this group from the others. On the whole this group seemed reasonably happy with the present regime despite reservations about the hardness of the work and the deterrent value of the regime.

Cluster III (n=7)

4.86 Members of this group were very impressed by the closeness of supervision within the centre, by the standards required and by the quality of the trainee response. More than any other group they thought the work suitably hard. By way of contrast they were doubtful about the place of education in the regime and were relatively unimpressed by the deterrent aspects of New Hall as it currently operated.

166

4.87 The views of this group were closely similar to those of Group I except for their more favourable view of the work and less favourable attitude towards education.

Cluster IV (n=6)
4.88 This group was by far the most critical of the regime. They held the poorest opinion of the place of education and saw little about the new regime that was hard or potentially an effective deterrent. They felt that the work was not hard and that most trainees would derive little benefit from their stay at New Hall. Although their views on the standards required, the closeness of supervision and trainees response were, on balance, favourable they were more moderate than those of the other groups. Group IV contains a hard core of opinion unimpressed by the new regime, dissatisfied, in particular, with its softness, the easiness of the work and the continued presence of education as an element within the working day.

Overall

4.89 Despite the inevitable variability in the responses, there was considerable agreement on a number of scales. Most evaluated supervision, standards and the response of the trainees highly; very few, however, considered the regime tough or likely to prove an effective deterrent. Opinions differed about the hardness of the work or the likelihood of trainees deriving benefit from their experience and were sharply divided over the place of education within the regime.

At Send

Cluster I (n=7)
4.90 This group is characterised by having the most negative views about the deterrent quality of

the regime (the standards required, the level of
supervision), and the most pessimistic opinion of
the long term benefit to the trainees of the
activities in the detention centre. Only the
members of cluster IV hold more negative views
about the hardness of the work.

Cluster II (n=10)
4.91 This group comprises those who hold the
highest opinion of the place of education in the
regime and a very positive view of the standards
required of trainees. They are more divided about
the hardness and toughness of the regime. They
are perhaps best described as those who believe
that the centre is largely working as was
intended, that standards of tidiness and
discipline are high, that trainees work hard, that
education has a place in the detention centre,
that activities are of benefit to the trainees,
but with some reservations about the deterrent
effect of the regime. A moderate group, in favour
of a mixed regime.

Cluster III (n=5)
4.92 More than any other group, the members of
this cluster believe the regime at Send to be
hard, demanding and tough and that it effectively
deters trainees from further offending. They are
also largely agreed that inspections are thorough,
that discipline and tidiness are emphasised and
that drill is properly conducted. They are
divided about the physical hardness of many of the
work tasks and are doubtful whether education
sessions are conducted in a way which reflects the
general tone and tempo of the establishment. This
group could perhaps best be described as including
those staff who think that the regime is operating
as intended, more strict but balanced.

Cluster IV (n=5)
4.93 This group is similar in most respects to the
members of Cluster III and merge with them at the
next level of clustering. However, despite their
positive response regarding most of the demanding
aspects of the new regime, they have doubts about
whether the experience really is tough or
deterring. None of them considered that the
education classes are conducted in such a way as
to reflect the tone and tempo of the
establishment.

5. TRAINEES' REACTIONS

INTRODUCTION

5.1 This chapter examines trainees' experience of the detention centre environment and their conduct within it. It seeks to ascertain whether the new regimes have a distinctive effect on trainees' experience and behaviour whilst in detention centre. This topic is important because it can give us clues as to the kind of regimes that have actually resulted from the attempt to implement the Note of Guidance at Send and New Hall. American research in particular has suggested that official descriptions of custodial regimes need to be supplemented by descriptions from the perspectives of inmates and staff (Moos, 1975; Quay, 1977).

5.2 Published research into trainees' experience in detention centre has seldom risen above the anecdotal level. Of more substance is the unpublished work of two former prison psychologists, Fuller and Reynolds. This work will be described in some detail both because it provides a depiction of how senior detention centres were experienced prior to the introduction of the pilot regimes[1] and because the techniques used to investigate trainees' experiences formed the basis for our own methodology. Fuller and Reynolds developed a card-sorting task as a standardised means of questioning trainees about their experiences in detention centre. Each card presented a specific question and two possible answers to it. The trainee was asked to sort the card into one of two piles to indicate the answer he chose. This method was claimed to hold

---

[1] These surveys were carried out in 1977.

trainees' attention better than an ordinary
questionnaire. The questions themselves were
selected on the basis of informal conversations
with trainees and staff. Data were collected on
288 trainees aged 17 to 20 serving a three month
detention centre sentence. Independent samples of
trainees (N=36) were interviewed at four different
stages of sentence (first week, third week, fifth
week, seventh week) in each of two senior
detention centres. Responses to questions were
analysed in terms of the degree of agreement
amongst trainees and the way in which answers
differed across the four stages of sentence. The
results of these analyses were used to build the
following picture of trainees' adjustment to
detention centre:-

In the initial stages of his sentence (ie
arrival and induction phases) the trainee
undergoes a rapid and relatively intense
process of adaptation to a new and strange
environment. A fair degree of personal
stress, insecurity and uncertainty is
experienced at this time. This is reflected
in his moods; in a certain inability to
accept, comprehend or cope with the regime
and its demands; confused and wary attitudes
towards the staff, and a good deal of remorse
coupled with 'motivation to change'.
Generally speaking, however, he does not show
extreme symptoms of stress and will recognise
the reasonable authority of the staff. At
the same time he is rapidly absorbing
information about his fellow inmates and the
informal or 'subcultural' aspects of the
institution.

By about the third week of his sentence a
significant acclimatisation has taken place.
Much of the uncertainty about the institution
has been resolved, he now feels more 'at

home' with the routine which is no longer
seen as particularly demanding or stern, and
his general mood is much lighter. His
increasing confidence in his ability to
manage his surroundings is expressed in a
more forward and positive attitude to staff
(with reservations), and also by a growth of
deviant behaviour. His discrimination of
friend and foe amongst his peers develops
fairly quickly, and while he may participate
in some of the usual institutional 'fiddles'
and skylarking, there is a limit to his
allegiance to other young offenders.

Very little of note marks out the fifth week
of custody, ie the point at which the halfway
'watershed' has just been passed. The
trainee is now, it seems, well acclimatised
to the regime and reconciled to serving the
remainder of his sentence without any
particular difficulty, and even though being
confined is not entirely without some stress
he may even be able to compensate for his
predicament by identifying some positive
benefits of being in DC, eg he feels much
fitter than he used to. On the whole his
relations with staff continue to improve, but
his institutional deviance is well in
evidence, possibly reaching a 'ceiling' at
about this time.

As the date of his release approaches in the
seventh week a few further adjustments occur
though these do not really override or negate
what has gone before. His mood continues to
lighten and the prospect of release may even
generate mild symptoms such as slight loss of
appetite, insomnia and a sense of dragging
time. Except perhaps for the odd 'final
fling', his rule-breaking and other deviance
does not increase noticeably; indeed, he may

curb some of his more easily detectable
transgressions. He may begin to disengage
from his sentence by perceiving the
institution and his fellow inmates in a less
favourable light, although his relations with
staff are not affected markedly either way.

5.3 Later research by Fuller (also unpublished)
replicated the original results and explored the
effects of various changes in methodology (eg
using repeated interviews with one group of
trainees at different points in their sentence
rather than interviewing independent groups;
interviewing trainees serving six month sentences
rather than just three months; analysing groups of
items related to the same topic (scales)[2] rather
than individual items etc). The results of these
various analyses confirmed Fuller and Reynolds'
original conclusions. The scales derived by
Fuller and Reynolds were modified by the Young
Offender Psychology Unit so as to be suitable for
use in borstal as well as detention centre and
they were further refined using various
statistical techniques (item analysis, factor
analysis), and a number of checks were made on
their validity[3]. Another prison psychologist,
McEwan, then applied these scales to samples of
trainees drawn from a junior detention centre.
His results were markedly similar to those
obtained by Fuller and Reynolds. Thus stress

---

[2] These scales were derived a priori and then refined
through factor analysis.

[3] Validity, ie the extent to which the scales actually
measure what they purport to measure. The results of
validity studies are summarised in Note 5.1 at the end of
this chapter.

(feelings of anxiety, fear, disorientation, being unable to cope) appeared to be high in samples of newly received trainees but was much lower for samples who had been in for three weeks or more. Deviance (rule-breaking, fighting, theft, vandalism) was lower immediately after reception than it was later in sentence. And trainees' attitude towards staff (the degree to which they saw staff as fair and benevolent) became gradually more positive during the course of the sentence.

5.4 Two aspects of this depiction of trainees' experiences in detention centre are particularly striking. First, except for an initial period of disorientation (the first couple of weeks) trainees do not appear to find detention centre particularly stressful. Indeed by the third week a substantial proportion of trainees would seem to characterise themselves as having an easy time. This should not necessarily be taken to indicate that they enjoy themselves[4]. Rather it suggests that they have learned how to cope with the demands placed on them in detention centre and no longer experience the regime as stretching. Of course not all trainees will experience detention centre in the same way. For some trainees it may be a continuously frightening experience, but this is rare. Second, detention centre training does not appear to suppress trainees' delinquency entirely. A considerable body of petty delinquency (fighting, vandalism, theft) takes place within detention centres, and the extent to which trainees engage in this seems to increase during the course of training. In one sense this is not very surprising, and the behaviour in itself is not very serious. After all detention

---

[4] Although in the early days of detention centres a Report of Commissioners of Prisons (1956) claimed that physical education, at least, is enjoyed by detention centre trainees.

centre trainees are convicted offenders and so
they might well be expected to continue to behave
in a delinquent fashion even within the custodial
environment. On the other hand it has been
suggested that delinquent behaviour established
within an institution may show some persistence
after release (Sinclair and Clarke, 1982).

5.5 It is not clear whether the pilot regimes
were introduced with the intention of modifying
these two aspects of existing regimes. However
consideration of the Note of Guidance does suggest
that some changes in these areas might be hoped
for. Specifically it is clear that the pilot
regimes were meant to be more rigorous and
demanding than ordinary regimes. The Note of
Guidance does not explicitly state that the pilot
regimes should be experienced as more stressful,
indeed it contains specific cautions against the
sort of staff practice which might be highly
stressful for trainees (Appendix A paragraph
A.37). However if demands are imposed in a more
rigorous fashion then at least some trainees are
likely to find it more difficult to meet them and
thus find the regime more stressful. Moreover,
even if the pilot regimes are not experienced as
more stressful it is reasonable to suggest that
the notion of a more demanding regime should at
least imply that the proportion of trainees who
feel they are having an easy time should diminish.

5.6 With regard to the second aspect, delinquency
engaged in within detention centres, the Note of
Guidance specifies that greater emphasis is to be
placed on discipline. It is not clear though
whether this is expected to lead to less
delinquency. It is easy to impose high standards
with regard to overt behaviour (eg such things as
neatness or politeness) but delinquent behaviours
such as theft or vandalism tend to be engaged in
covertly and so are less amenable to direct staff

control. It is still possible, however, that the pilot regimes might reduce the level of delinquent behaviour engaged in within detention centre. The Note of Guidance specifies that raised standards are to be achieved, not by direct punitive control, but by staff example and the more general effects of the regime. If successfully applied such indirect modes of influence might affect covert as well as overt behaviour and so lead to reduced levels of delinquency within the centres.

5.7 There are obvious dangers entailed by the implementation of 'tougher' regimes. The regime might become harshly punitive, eliciting in trainees either terror or resentment. The Note of Guidance appears alive to these dangers, specifically cautioning staff against unprofessional escalation of standards of discipline, and suggesting that 'the interest taken by staff in the progress and well-being of trainees ....[is to]..... be a focal part of the project'. Thus the intention was clearly to avoid a harshly punitive regime developing.

5.8 The combination of firmness and fairness, of strictness and interest in trainees' well-being, specified by the Note of Guidance, is one which has long been held as an ideal within detention centres. Researchers, too, have suggested that it is this combination which produces the best results, both in terms of behaviour within custodial institutions and perhaps in terms of behaviour after release (Sinclair and Clarke, 1982). This same research indicates however that the desired combination is rather rare. Regimes which are strict and firm tend to manifest less kindness, and regimes which are kind and fair tend to be more permissive (Sinclair 1975; Moos, 1975). This does not mean that it is impossible to achieve the desired combination, since, although relatively rare, such regimes were found.

176

5.9 In the light of this research, therefore, an
important possibility existed that the pilot
regimes at Send and New Hall would turn out in
practice either to be strict, rigorous and
demanding but harsh and punitive, or fair and kind
but no more rigorous and demanding than ordinary
detention centre regimes.

METHODOLOGY

Data Collection

5.10 Once during period I and once during period
II (ie before and after the introduction of the
new regimes) we attempted to interview
individually all trainees held in the pilot and
comparison centres (these 'occupation samples' are
described in chapter two). During these
interviews trainees were questioned about their
experience and behaviour in detention centres.
This information was then supplemented by
examining trainees' records after they had been
discharged to determine the number of times they
had been put on disciplinary report and the amount
of remission lost.

5.11 The procedure used to question trainees was
based on that employed by Fuller and Reynolds.
Trainees were required to sort a deck of cards
into two piles, an 'A' pile and a 'B' pile. Each
card bore a single statement or question with two
possible responses, one marked 'A' and the other
'B'. Trainees were asked to read each card aloud
and then sort it into either the 'A' pile or the
'B' pile depending upon which response they had
selected. Trainees who showed difficulty in
reading had the items read to them by the
interviewer. All interviews were preceeded by an
explanation of the research and an assurance that
the trainees' answers were confidential. Thirty-
seven of the questions were grouped into three

scales: Stress, Attitude to Staff and Deviance.
Since these are unpublished scales, evidence
bearing on their validity and reliability is
summarised in Note 5.1 at the end of this chapter.
The scales should not be regarded as 'a test',
rather they offer trainees a systematic and
standardised way of communicating about their
experience and conduct in detention centres. The
evidence summarised in Note 5.1 suggests that the
trainees understand the questions, that their
answers can be summarised in terms of these three
dimensions, and that trainees are reasonably
truthful in the answers that they give. The three
dimensions can be summarised as follows:

i.   Stress: a trainee scoring high on Stress
      depicts himself as feeling unhappy,
      frightened, tense, irritable, etc. A trainee
      scoring low on Stress depicts himself as
      feeling relaxed and as having an easy time in
      detention centre. He denies the 'signs' of
      high stress. The Stress items focus on the
      trainees reactions inside the detention
      centre.

ii.   Attitude to Staff: a trainee scoring high on
      Attitude to Staff depicts staff as caring,
      helpful, friendly, fair and easy to trust. A
      trainee scoring low on Attitude to Staff
      depicts staff as not having these
      characteristics.

iii. Deviance: a trainee scoring high on Deviance
      depicts himself as breaking the institution's
      rules and as engaging in various minor forms
      of delinquency (stealing, fighting,
      vandalism) whilst in detention centre. The
      items predominantly focus on the trainee's
      recent behaviour ('In the last week have you
      ......').

178

5.12 In addition to these three scales a number of supplementary questions were asked, two of which are analysed here. These were:- 'In the last few days has anyone tried to bully you or make fun of you in front of the other trainees?' 'In the last month has anything of yours been stolen in here?'

5.13 One item from the Stress scale ('Are you having an easy time in here now?') was picked out for separate analysis because it seemed particularly pertinent to the expected effects of the pilot regimes.

5.14 Finally, after trainees had been discharged their records were examined to establish the number of disciplinary reports that they had incurred and the amount of remission that this had cost.

Data analysis

5.15 Tables are presented which contrast the results obtained in period II with those obtained in period I separately for all six centres. The figures presented in these tables have all been adjusted so as to remove spurious differences arising from variation in the composition of the samples. A non-technical account of the statistical technique used to do this (analysis of covariance) is contained in the methodology section of Chapter 6. It is important however to note the technique's main limitation: it can only adjust for the effects of measured variables. A list of the variables the effects of which have been statistically adjusted for, using this technique, is contained in Note 5.2.

5.16 In analysing these tables we have first tested for statistically reliable differences between the results obtained in period II as opposed to period I. These tests were carried out separately for all six centres. In the case of New Hall and Send, new regimes were in force during period II but not during period I.

5.17 Thus, for these two centres the difference between results obtained in period I and those obtained in period II may reflect the introduction of the pilot regime. Differences between these two periods might reflect a number of other factors, however, including the time of year (period I data was collected at the end of September, period II data was collected in June and July), the prevailing weather conditions, the general social and economic climate etc. The importance of these factors is unknown, although both weather conditions and time of the year have been reported as affecting some forms of institutional behaviour (Clarke and Martin, 1971; Baron and Ransberger, 1978). In order to take some account of these factors we examine the difference in results between period I and II for the comparison establishments (which were running ordinary regimes during both periods).

5.18 If the change in results for Send and New Hall is different from that observed for the comparison centres then this suggests that at least a portion of the change in results for Send and New Hall is to be attributed to the introduction of the pilot regimes. If, on the other hand, there are changes in the results for Send and New Hall, but these are similar in size and direction to those observed at the comparison centres, then the change in the results observed at Send and New Hall cannot properly be attributed to the pilot regimes.

5.19 Three further complications have to be taken into account. First, the change produced by implementing the pilot regime at Send may have been different from the change produced by

implementing the pilot regime at New Hall. This
could arise for a variety of reasons. For
example, pre-existing differences between the Send
and New Hall regimes would provide a different
baseline against which the pilot regime was being
contrasted; junior trainees have different
requirements and may react differently from senior
trainees; and the different groups of staff might
have developed a different collective
interpretation of the Note of Guidance. To allow
for this complication we have analysed the results
for the junior centres separately from the results
for the senior centres.

5.20 The second complication is that the change
observed for the comparison centres may vary from
one centre to another. It is inevitable that this
will be true to some extent: some variation is to
be expected just on the basis of chance (sampling
error). For this reason we compare the change in
results observed for Send to a weighted average[7]
of the changes observed for the two junior
comparison centres. Equally, the change in
results observed for New Hall is compared with the
weighted average of the changes observed for the
two senior comparison centres. The results of
these comparisons are given in the tables that
follow under the heading 'estimated effect of
regime change'. This quantity can be interpreted
as the difference between the change at the
experimental centre (Send or New Hall) and the
weighted average change at the relevant comparison
establishments, (or more simply as the difference
between the results obtained under the pilot
regime and the results that would have been
expected for that establishment in period II had
the pilot regimes not been introduced).

---

[7]   Weighted so as to allow for sample size.

5.21 Whilst this quantity is designed to take account of chance variation in the size or direction of the changes observed for the comparison centres, it begins to lose its meaning if substantially different changes are observed at the comparison centres. In this case it is necessary to try to interpret the overall pattern of results. And it may be difficult to make confident inferences about the specific effect of introducing the pilot regime.

5.22 The third complication applies only to the senior establishments. Between periods I and II catchment areas changed for all the senior centres. The nature of these changes and possible ways of coping with them are described at the end of Chapter 2 in Note 2.2.

5.23 The methods vary in the degree to which they are subject to biases produced by the catchment area changes. Unfortunately freedom from potential catchment area bias is bought only at the expense of a reduced sample size (large numbers of cases having to be dropped for the most bias-free method). Thus we can have a relatively imprecise estimate of an unbiased statistic or a relatively precise estimate of a (possibly) biased statistic. Which of the three methods is to be preferred depends upon how likely it is that the catchment area changes would bias the results. Bias could be introduced in three main ways. First, the catchment area changes might alter the kinds of trainee received. We have however taken considerable care to equate statistically the samples on trainees characteristics so if this was the only effect of the catchment area change its importance would not be great. Second, the catchment area changes might alter the kind of area to which trainees are discharged. For example, many New Hall trainees in period II would have been returning to homes in the Manchester area whereas this was not so during period I. The effect is potentially of considerable significance for reconviction results but is probably less important for the analyses described in the present chapter since these latter relate to behaviour and reactions inside the detention centre. Third, the catchment area changes might alter the degree to which regional rivalries or antagonisms are invoked inside the institutions. Neither the psychologist observer at New Hall nor the staff (when interviewed) reported an increase in such rivalries. Thus it seems likely that only a relatively small amount of bias would have been introduced.

5.24 We therefore decided to employ method B (which provides moderate protection against catchment area bias and a reasonable degree of precision) as the primary technique. The results for the senior detention centre data which appear in the tables in the following section are based on this technique. We have however carried out parallel analyses using method C, which provides less protection against bias but allows us to use a larger sample and so gives more precise estimates. The issue does not arise for the junior centres.

5.25 Where there is some discrepancy between the results obtained with the two procedures we comment on this. These discrepancies can take two forms. The first is a change in the strength or direction of the estimated effect of regime change which we interpret as probably reflecting the result of some bias introduced by the catchment area changes (and accordingly rely on the results of method B which more fully removes such biases). The second is a relatively unchanged estimate of the effect of regime change which is more statistically significant when method C is used. We interpret this as reflecting the reduced

precision of the results in method B and
accordingly rely on the results of method C.

5.26 Technical details of the statistical analysis
are given in Note 5.3 at the end of this chapter.

RESULTS AND DISCUSSION

The junior trainees

5.27 Tables 5.1a and 5.1b display the main results
for the junior centres. The introduction of the
pilot regime at Send was associated with two
statistically reliable changes: trainees'
attitudes towards staff became more positive (ie
they were more likely to describe staff as being
fair and benevolent) and the average number of
times trainees incurred disciplinary reports
increased substantially. Both these changes at
Send were not only reliably different from zero
but they were also reliably different from the
changes occurring in the comparison centres[8]. In
addition there was a suggestion that bullying
might have declined as a result of the
introduction of the pilot regime. This apparent
trend was, however, of only marginal reliability
and actually appears more by way of a contrast
between Send and Campsfield House than as a
straightforward change at Send.

5.28 The introduction of the pilot regime was not
associated with statistically reliable changes in

---

[8] The picture is slightly complicated in the case of
discipline reports because there was also a statistically
significant change at Campsfield. This change was however
in the opposite direction to that observed at Send. In
addition, the change at Send was significantly different
from the change at the other comparison centre.

the amount of delinquency trainees reported
engaging in within detention centre; the frequency
with which they reported having had their property
stolen; the level of stress experienced by
trainees; or the proportion of trainees who
described themselves as having an easy time.
Changes at Send in the levels of these variables
were not only not statistically reliable, they
were also small relative to the amount of
variation that naturally occurs amongst trainees
within a detention centre.

5.29 The regime at Campsfield House, one of the
comparison centres, appears to have changed
substantially on a number of dimensions of trainee
experience. Specifically members of the period I
Campsfield House sample reported more stress, less
often described themselves as having an easy time,
less often reported having their possessions
stolen within detention centre and were put on
disciplinary report more often. In these respects
the period I Campsfield sample differed not only
from the period II Campsfield House sample but
also from most of the other junior samples.

5.30 In contrast the regime at the other junior
comparison centre (Eastwood Park) appears to have
been experienced in a remarkably similar way in
the two periods, the only statistically reliable
change being a reduction in the proportion of
trainees who reported having their possessions
stolen.

5.31 At all three junior centres the nature of
trainees' experiences seems to depend upon how
long they had been in the centre. For example,
trainees within the first fortnight reported
substantially more stress. The other changes
described by Fuller and Reynolds (see paragraph
5.2 above) were also apparent. Particularly

Table 5.1(a) Junior trainees' custodial adjustment

Detention centre	Send		Eastwood Park	
Period Regime	I Ordinary	II Pilot	I Ordinary	II Ordinary
Mean score on Stress (a high score expresses unhappiness, fear, tension, irritability etc)	5.10	5.19	5.23	5.13
Mean score on Attitude to Staff (a high score expresses a positive attitude towards staff)	5.74	6.64*[9]	5.99	6.22
Mean score on Deviance (a high score expresses a large amount of theft, fighting, vandalism and rule-breaking)	2.51	2.04	2.43	1.97

[9] Asterisks appearing in the period II column indicate that I result for the same centre. The number of asterisks

[10] The 'estimated effect of regime change' column shows deviate from those which would have been expected to occur introduced.

[11] The 'within-sample standard deviation' is an index of occurring within a centre on any particular occasion. background against which any difference between samples can third the size of the within-sample standard deviation may naturally occurring within detention centres. It is not to of the overall effect.

[12] 'Statistical significance' refers to the probability of an or larger than that observed if there was really no effect.

Campsfield House		estimated[10] effect of regime change	within[11] sample standard deviation	statistical[12] significance
I Ordinary	II Ordinary			
7.19	5.35*[9]	+1.06	3.53	Not significant
6.44	5.58	+1.21	2.41	0.0286
1.31	1.47	-0.32	1.77	Not significant

the period II result is reliably different from the period
denotes the significance level involved (*=5%, **=1%, ***=0.1%).

the degree to which the results for the pilot regime
for that centre in period II had the pilot regime not been

the average amount of variation between trainees
See note 5.4 at the end of this chapter. It provides a
be assessed: a difference which is less than (say) one
be regarded as being small relative to the variation
be confused with the standard error of the mean score or

'estimated effect of regime change' occurring as large
Probabilities greater than 0.1 are shown as 'not significant'.

Table 5.1(b) Junior trainees' custodial adjustment

Detention centre	Send		Eastwood Park	
Period	I	II	I	II
Regime	Ordinary	Pilot	Ordinary	Ordinary
Percent having an easy time ('Are you having an easy time in here now? Yes/No')	59%	52%	51%	54%
Percent victim of theft ('In the last month has anything of yours been stolen in here? Yes/No')	52%	42%	44%	23%[*9]
Percent bullied ('In the last few days has anyone tried to bully you or make fun of you in front of the other trainees? Yes/No')	31%	22%	22%	23%
Mean number of disciplinary reports	0.53	0.95[**9]	0.16	0.15
Mean number of days remission lost	1.39	2.01	0.18	0.26

188

Campsfield House		estimated[10] effect of regime change	statistical[12] significance
I Ordinary	II Ordinary		
35%	65%[**9]	-22%	0.0375
14%	44%[**9]	-15%	Not significant
12%	28%	-18%	0.0615
1.55	0.33[***9]	+1.03	0.0001
0.58	0.23	+0.76	Not significant

striking were the changes during the course of a sentence in the proportion of trainees who reported themselves to be having an easy time. At Send less than a third of trainees interviewed during their first two weeks reported having an easy time. For trainees interviewed after their fourth week the proportion was about two-thirds.

5.32 A surprising feature of the results for Send was that the substantial difference between period I and period II in the number of disciplinary reports incurred was accompanied by only a rather small difference in the average amount of remission lost. This suggest that the 'extra' reports incurred under the pilot regime may have been for rather minor infractions. The results of a subsidiary analysis confirm this inference, as follows.

5.33 All disciplinary reports at Send during the period May to September 1979 (before the introduction of the pilot regime) and the period May to September 1980 (after it had been introduced) were categorised in terms of seriousness. The table below displays the result.

Table 5.2 Disciplinary reports at Send: May to September 1979 and 1980

	Less serious	More serious
1979	64	78
1980	211	75

The following offences were categorised as 'More serious': fighting, assault on staff, absconding, smoking, taxing/receiving, and self-injury. The distinction between more and less serious offences was made prior to inspection of the data.

5.34 The pilot regime was associated with a substantially larger number of minor infractions but the number of major infractions was more or less unchanged.

5.35 We have considered two possible interpretations of this result. There may have been a genuine increase in the number of minor infractions or staff may have more often responded to minor infractions by putting the trainee on disciplinary report. There are some grounds for preferring the second interpretation. Self-reported deviance did not increase. This is not compelling though since the self-report items focussed predominantly on items that would have been categorised as 'more serious' infractions. However, staff themselves would surely have known if the increased number of discipline reports for minor infractions had reflected a genuine deterioration in trainees' behaviour and when asked about this (as part of the first survey of staff opinion described in chapter four) they did not suggest that trainee behaviour had deteriorated.

The senior trainees

5.36 Tables 5.3a and 5.3b display the main results for the senior centres. The introduction of the pilot regime at New Hall was associated with four statistically reliable changes: trainees' attitudes towards staff became more positive (this effect was even more marked than at Send), the amount of stress experienced by trainees became substantially less, the proportion of trainees saying that they were having an easy time was very much higher, and the proportion reporting that their property had been stolen fell somewhat. The changes observed at New Hall for the first two variables (attitude to staff and stress) were not only statistically reliable in themselves but were

Table 5.3(a) Senior trainees' custodial adjustment

Detention centre	New Hall		Buckley Hall	
Period	I	II	I	II
Regime	Ordinary	Pilot	Ordinary	Ordinary
Mean score on Stress (a high score expresses unhappiness, fear, tension,	7.02	3.58 ***9	3.63	4.20
Mean score on Attitude to Staff (a high score expresses a positive attitude towards staff)	4.87	7.04 ***9	6.10	5.43
Mean score on Deviance (a high score expresses a large amount of theft, fighting, vandalism and rule-breaking)	2.72	2.26	3.40	3.40

9 Asterisks appearing in the period II column indicate that result for the same centre. The number of asterisks denote

10 The 'estimated effect of regime change' column shows the those which would have been expected to occur for that centre

11 The 'within-sample standard deviation' is an index of the a centre on any particular occasion. See Note 5.4 at the end any difference between samples can be assessed: a difference sample, standard deviation may be regarded as being small centres.

12 'Statistical significance' refers to the probability of an larger than that observed if there was really no effect.

Werrington House		estimated[10] effect of regime change	within[11] sample standard deviation	statistical[12] significance
I Ordinary	II Ordinary			
3.37	5.05	−4.65	3.33	0.0001
8.37	7.49	+2.97	2.11	0.0001
2.25	1.79	−0.03	1.90	Not significant

the period II result is reliably different from the period I
the significant level involved (*=5%, **=1%, ***=0.1%).

degree to which the results for the pilot regime deviate from
in period II had the pilot regime not been introduced.

average amount of variation between trainees occurring within
of this chapter. It provides a background against which
which is less than (say) one third the size of the within-
relative to the variation naturally occurring within detention

'estimated effect of regime change' occurring as large or
Probabilities greater than 0.1 are shown as 'not significant'.

Table 5.3(b) Senior trainees' custodial adjustment

Detention centre	New Hall		Buckley Hall	
Period Regime	I Ordinary	II Pilot	I Ordinary	II Ordinary
Percent having an easy time ('Are you having an easy time in here? Yes/No')	39%	67%[*9]	74%	78%
Percent victim of theft ('In the last month has anything of yours been stolen in here? Yes/No')	66%	43%[*9]	93%	68%
Percent bullied ('In the last few days has anyone tried to bully you or make fun of you in front of the other trainees? Yes/No')	30%	14%	30%	34%
Mean number of disciplinary reports	0.24	0.58	0.23	0.35
Mean number of days remission lost	0.46	1.13	1.31	1.86

Werrington House		estimated[10] effect of regime change	statistical[12] significance
I Ordinary	II Ordinary		
64%	58%	+30%	0.0703
71%	73%	−14%	Not significant
48%	23%	−3%	Not significant
1.29	0.97	+0.47	Not significant
1.24	0.78	+0.69	Not significant

reliably different from the average changes at the senior comparison centres. The change at New Hall in the proportion of trainees who described themselves as having an easy time, whilst statistically reliable in itself, was not clearly reliably different from the changes occuring at the comparison centres. This result was obtained using method B to control for possible bias introduced by catchment area changes. When however method C is used, then the difference between the change for New Hall and the average change for the comparison centres was statistically reliable. The reason for this discrepancy was not that method C produced a larger estimate of the difference in changes. The discrepancy arose solely because of the more precise estimates obtainable with method C. Following the principle articulated in the data analysis section we therefore infer that the change for New Hall in the proportion of trainees saying they were having an easy time may be regarded as being reliably different from the changes observed for the comparison centres.

5.37 The situation is somewhat different with regard to the proportion of trainees who report having had their property stolen. Although there was a statistically reliable change in this proportion for New Hall, this change was not reliably different from that observed for the comparison centres. In fact the change observed at Buckley Hall was of similar magnitude to that observed at New Hall[13]. This makes it difficult to be confident that the change observed at New

---

[13] The change at Buckley Hall was not statistically reliable despite being of similar size to that at New Hall. This is because the New Hall samples were larger, thus allowing more precise estimates.

Hall was due to the pilot regime as opposed to some more general influence which affected both Buckley Hall and New Hall. The change at Buckley Hall does however reflect a very high theft level reported by the period I Buckley Hall sample. The level of theft reported by trainees at New Hall under the pilot regime is lower than that reported by any other senior sample[14].

5.38 The introduction of the pilot regime at New Hall was not associated with statistically reliable changes in the amount of delinquency trainees reported engaging in within detention centre, the proportion of trainees who reported that they had been bullied, or the number of disciplinary reports incurred or the amount of remission lost.

5.39 In contrast with the results for junior comparison centres, neither of the senior comparison centres showed statistically reliable differences between period I and period II. In part this may have been because of smaller sample sizes. However examination of the actual figures shows that none of the changes for the senior comparison centre were of the same order as those observed for Campsfield House.

5.40 Like the junior centre data, however, the senior centre data also showed that the nature of trainees' experience depended upon how far through their sentence they were. Again this was most dramatically apparent for stress which appeared to be much higher for trainees interviewed during their first two weeks than it was for trainees interviewed later in their sentences.

---

[14] It differs reliably from three of the samples, and almost reliably (p greater than 0.05 but less than 0.10) from the other two.

5.41 A similarly striking trend was apparent for the proportion of trainees who described themselves as having an easy time. For example, under the pilot regime at New Hall, whereas less than half of the trainees interviewed during their first two weeks described themselves as having an easy time, over four fifths of those interviewed after the fourth week did so.

CONCLUSIONS AND GENERAL DISCUSSION

Conclusions with regard to trainees' experience

5.42 In paragraphs 5.8 and 5.9 above it was suggested that implementation of the pilot project might shift the regimes at Send and New Hall in any of three directions. That is, they might have moved in the direction of a regime experienced as strict and demanding but basically fair and benevolent; a regime experienced as frightening and harshly punitive; or a regime experienced as benevolent but undemanding.

5.43 In the event, at New Hall implementation of the pilot project seems to have shifted the regime in the third direction: staff were perceived as fairer and more benevolent; trainees reported experiencing less stress; and a higher proportion of them claimed to be having an easy time when they were interviewed.

5.44 The pattern at Send was more complex. It might be argued that Send changed in the first direction, as being strict and demanding but basically fair and benevolent. The increased use of discipline reports might be taken to indicate greater strictness. And since the proportion of trainees reporting that they were having an easy time when interviewed declined slightly at Send but increased in both the junior comparison centres, this might be taken to indicate that the

implementation of the pilot project made the Send
regime more demanding. Finally, the trainees'
more positive attitudes towards staff indicates
that staff were perceived as fairer and more
benevolent.

5.45 There are certain problems in interpreting
the results in this way. The increased use of
disciplinary reports at Send may reflect, not
increased strictness but an increased use of
formal (rather than informal) punishments for the
less serious infractions. The contrast between
Send and the comparison centres in the proportion
of trainees who reported having an easy time is
actually due to a substantial change in this
proportion for Campsfield House. The figures for
Send and for the other comparison centre are in
fact fairly similar for the two periods. Thus the
data do not really support the suggestion that the
Send regime became more demanding with the
implementation of the pilot project.

Conclusions with regard to trainees' conduct

5.46 Although implementing the pilot regimes seems
to have affected the way in which Send and New
Hall were experienced by trainees, it does not
seem to have much improved trainees' conduct
within the centres. The increase in disciplinary
reports might be taken to indicate that trainees'
conduct had actually deteriorated. However, we
have argued that this reflects a change in staff
behaviour rather than an increase in rule-breaking
by the trainees. This contention is supported by
three sources of information: trainees' reports of
their own delinquent behaviour in the centres;
trainees' reports of the extent to which they have
been the victim of delinquent behaviour within the
centre; and staff perceptions of trainees'
behaviour.

5.47 In fact, if one disregards the increase in disciplinary reports, all the other indices of trainees' behaviour suggest that the introduction of both pilot regimes was associated with a very slight improvement in their conduct. Although these trends were consistent across the three measures which were independent of staff behaviour (self-reported deviance, percent reporting having their property stolen, and percent being bullied) and across both junior and senior establishments, they were so weak that in most instances they could have arisen by chance. Thus the most we can safely conclude is that there may have been a slight improvement in trainees' conduct.

DISCUSSION

5.48 This section considers possible interpretations of the results reported in this chapter, several aspects of which are sufficiently striking to require explanation.

5.49 Both senior and junior pilot regimes seem to have induced in trainees more positive attitudes towards staff. This change is consistent with emphases within the Note of Guidance which specified that 'all staff should maintain a personal interest in individuals, and encourage trainees to seek counsel, advice and support ...' and further that staff 'will be firm but fair. The interest taken by staff in the progress and well-being of trainees will be a focal part of the project'. And the Note goes on to say that 'staff should themselves take pride in and uphold the prison service's high professional standards, and set an irreproachable example'. Now if, as a result of these injunctions, staff did all these things to a greater extent than hitherto trainees might be expected to become more inclined to describe staff as being more caring, helpful, friendly, fair and easy to trust (which is what is

involved in a more positive attitude to staff).
The problem is that most of the Note of Guidance's
prescriptions correspond to standard good practice
in detention centres. Thus wardens have been
emphasising the 'firm but fair' demeanour of staff
since detention centres were introduced and staff
at Send and New Hall tended to use this phrase to
describe their method of handling trainees both
before and after the introduction of the new
regime. Indeed the prescriptions in the Note of
Guidance do themselves seem more concerned to see
that an existing staff practice was not eroded by
the new regime rather than to introduce some
change. Why then were trainees' attitudes to
staff so markedly more positive under the pilot
regime? There are a number of possibilities, all
of which may have been operative.

5.50 First, the idea of implementing a 'tough'
regime may have raised the spectre of staff's
behaviour being interpreted as brutal. This could
have led staff to take more care over how they
treated trainees. It is not clear how plausible
this speculation is. Some such effect is apparent
in the Note of Guidance itself (ie the Note is
careful to emphasise the need to avoid what are
referred to as 'unprofessional or unauthorised
staff practices'). However neither the
psychologist-observers at Send and New Hall, nor
the staff when interviewed, reported the sort of
change in the methods employed by staff which
would correspond to this.

5.51 Second, staff's behaviour towards trainees
may not have changed but it may have been
differently evaluated in the context of coming to
a special 'tough' detention centre at which staff
might (in the popular mind) be expected to be
particularly brutal. We have no evidence that
bears on the plausibility of this hypothesis.

5.52 Third, trainees' experience of staff may have been more positive because the changed activities under the pilot regime led to a greater frequency of pleasant interactions between staff and trainees. For example, activities like drill and parades were administered in a comparatively sympathetic and patient fashion and gave trainees many opportunities to win staff approval. This third explanation seems to us the most plausible.

5.53 The second set of results to require explanation are those for stress and for the proportion of trainees who reported that they were having an easy time. Two points actually seem to need explanation here: why did neither pilot regime appear to be substantially more demanding than the ordinary regimes; and why was stress lower and the proportion of trainees reporting having an easy time higher after the pilot regime had been implemented at New Hall. One possibility is that both regimes actually became more demanding but that bravado stimulated by being in a 'tough' regime led trainees to claim that they were having an easy time when in fact they were not. It is difficult to see, however, why bravado should have been particularily operative at New Hall rather than at Send. Moreover, neither the psychologist-observers nor the consensus of staff opinion at the two institutions depicted the trainees as finding the pilot regimes harder. Indeed the consensus of staff opinion at New Hall was that the regime had become easier for trainees. The consensus of staff opinion at Send was that there had been no change in this respect. Thus there was a clear correspondence between the depiction of the changes derived from staff and the depiction of the changes derived from trainees. Since the trainees' accounts of how hard they found the regime tally with other sources of information we are inclined to take

them at face value. The other possibility is that
the change in activities involved in the pilot
regimes was not of a kind that would make these
regimes more demanding. As was noted above,
activities like drill and parades which were given
special emphasis under the pilot regimes were
administered in a sympathetic fashion and
consequently were comparatively popular with
trainees. Physical education, which was also
emphasised under the pilot regimes, is known to be
popular with many young offenders and perhaps
appeals to the 'tough', 'machismo' element in
delinquent subcultures. It is conceivable that
physical education might be run in a way that
would be highly demanding (pushing trainees to the
point of exhaustion etc) but this is quite
contrary to accepted philosophy and standards for
physical education, and in any case such practices
were specifically prohibited by the Note of
Guidance. Similarly, inspections are only likely
to be found demanding if trainees have difficulty
in passing them, whereas, in practice, the
trainees were carefully taught all that was
required. Finally, the pilot regime was supposed
to involve a particular emphasis on hard physical
work. But the consensus amongst staff (who saw
trainees engaged in the various tasks) was that
there were few tasks of this kind.

5.54 This basic notion that it is the nature of
the activities that were introduced that explains
trainees' reactions can be extended to account for
the different reactions observed at Send and New
Hall. At New Hall the 'new' activities (drill,
extra physical education etc) reduced the amount
of time spent on work. Work tended to be less
popular than these new activities, hence the
change involved the displacement of a relatively
unpopular activity by a relatively popular one.
This may account for trainees finding the pilot
regime at New Hall easier and less stressful than
the regime it replaced.

5.55 The argument in both this and the preceeding paragraph depends upon assertions about how trainees experienced particular activities. To test these a supplementary survey was carried out at Send and New Hall in October 1980. All trainees in each regime were asked to classify various activities according to whether they liked or disliked them. Table 5.4 displays the results for drill, parades, physical education and inspections at Send, the lower panel giving the results for various forms of work.

Table 5.4 Percentage liking various activities at Send

Drill/parades		Physical education		Kit/ inspections	
Morning parade	36%	Circuit training	58%	Folding kit	47%
Lunchtime drill parade	46%	Weight training	88%	Cleaning boots	47%
Practising drill	46%	Gymnastics	75%	Preparing for warden's inspection	54%
Warden's drill inspection	56%				

Work activities			
Spreading manure	9%	Sweeping	38%
Working in tunnels	28%	Working in laundry	55%
Working in fields	30%	Cleaning dormitory	45%
Raking big fields	24%	Cleaning recesses	10%
Weeding big flower beds	36%	Cutting logs	46%

5.56 Table 5.5 displays the corresponding results for New Hall.

Table 5.5 Percentage liking various actitives at New Hall

Drill/parades		Physical education		Kit/ inspections	
Morning parade	49%	Circuit training	72%	Tidying dormitory for inspection	42%
Afternoon drill	40%	Games and PE at weekends	82%	Warden's inspection on Saturday mornings	36%
Sunday parade	47%	Gymnastics	78%		
		PE exercises with medicine balls and benches	73%		

Work activities			
Scrubbing the main corridor	10%	Milking cows and cleaning dairy	65%
Digging in the compound	26%	Working in loomshop	25%
Cutting the grass	35%	Cleaning bath house reccesses	10%
Weeding flower beds	27%	Working in kitchen	80%

5.57 It can be seen that at least some of those activities which were newly introduced or emphasised under the pilot regime were relatively popular with trainees. This seems to have applied particularly to physical education but was also true of inspections, drills and parades. Work, time for which was reduced as a consequence of the introduction of the pilot regime at New Hall but not at Send, was generally quite unpopular with predictable exceptions such as working in the kitchen.

NOTES TO CHAPTER 5

Note 5.1 Validity and reliability of card-sort scales of Stress, Deviance and Attitude to Staff

5.58 There are no published data bearing on the validity and reliability of these scales. A good deal of unpublished research into their validity has, however, been carried out by prison psychologists (primarily by the Young Offender Psychology Unit). The scales' validity is supported by the results of factor analyses, studies using staff ratings, and studies using established psychometric measures of related constructs. The scales' main limitation is their length (10 items for the Attitude to Staff scale, 11 items for the Deviance scale, and 16 items for the Stress scale). This leads to correspondingly limited reliability coefficients, Cronbach's alpha coefficient being 0.71 for the Attitude to Staff scale, 0.65 for the Deviance scale and 0.80 for the Stress scale. The most important consequence of this limitation is that observed correlations with the scales will tend to be somewhat smaller than the true correlations.

5.59 A manual for these scales is currently under preparation within the Young Offender Psychology Unit.

Note 5.2 A list of the covariates used in the analyses reported in Chapter Five

1. Number of previous convictions: this refers to the number of distinct occasions on which the trainee had previously been convicted. It was coded into eight levels (0 through to 7 or more convictions).

2. Age on first conviction: in years

3. Number of convictions in the last two years at liberty

4. Any motor convictions (Yes=1; No=0)

5. Any summary convictions (Yes=1; No=0)

6. Any criminal damage convictions (Yes=1; No=0)

7. Any convictions for violence (Yes=1; No=0) (Robbery and sex offences and violence offences triable summarily only are not included.)

8. Any robbery convictions (Yes=1; No=0)

9. Any burglary convictions (Yes=1; No=0)

10. Any theft convictions (Yes=1; No=0)

11. Any fraud convictions (Yes=1; No=0)

12. Any previous detention centre sentences (Yes=1; No=0)

13. Months in local authority residential care

14. Ever remanded in custody (Yes=1; No=0)

15. Any supervision or probation order (Yes=1; No=0)

16. History of absconding: number of occasions absconded either from detention centre or from local authority residential care

17. Psychiatric contact: previous contact with a psychiatrist or a psychologist. Referrals on remand were excluded.

18. Self-injury: number of times tried to injury self

19. Age on sentence: in years

20. Height: in inches

21. Build (small/slight=1; other=0)

22. Black (black-skinned=1; other=0)

23. Other non-white (Other non-white=1; white or black=0)

24. Literate: whether or not was able to read the card-sort items

25. Similarities test: raw score on the similarities sub-test of the WAIS

26. Number of days since reception: both linear and quadratic components of this variable were included for all analyses except those of disciplinary reports and loss of remission

5.3 The statistical analyses

5.60 These were fixed effect analyses of covariance as implemented by the General Linear Model program from the SAS package (SAS Institute, 1982). Period and centre were defined as factors with covariates as listed in Note 5.2. The LSMEANS and PDIFF options were used to obtain adjusted means and to test (usually a priori) contrasts between them. The 'estimated effect of regime change' statistic was obtained by using the ESTIMATE option to partition the interaction effect.

5.61 Since a number of dependent variables had skewed distributions we investigated the effect of various alternative methods of analysis. For example, analysing the two dependent variables, percent of trainees with discipline reports, and number of discipline reports amongst those trainees having at least one, gave essentially similar results to those reported in the text. Additionally, results obtained with theoretically preferable procedures (logistic regression for dichotomous dependent variables) gave virtually identical estimates and significance levels to those obtained with ordinary least squares. Thus although some of the technical assumptions underlying analysis of covariance are violated in a number of instances, the effect of these violations seems to have been sufficiently small as not to be of practical importance.

Note 5.4 Within-sample standard deviations

5.62 These are the standard deviations of the residuals obtained when fitting a model containing only period, centre, and point in sentence effects. They may be thought of as indicating the average amount of variability amongst trainees within any given establishment at any particular point in their sentences.

5.63 This statistic is calculated only for card-sort scales. It is not meaningful for dichotomous variables. And it is less relevant for variables (such as number of days remission lost) which have an absolute interpretation.

6. RECONVICTIONS

INTRODUCTION

6.1 This chapter examines the rate at which trainees were reconvicted after their release from detention centre, and seeks to ascertain whether the pilot regimes had a distinctive effect on their reconviction rates. This bears on the primary goal of the pilot project, namely of assessing 'whether young offenders can be effectively deterred from committing further offences' by the pilot project regimes.

6.2 Reconviction is the most widely used criterion in studies evaluating the effectiveness of different methods of treating offenders. A great many of these, of different kinds, have been compared. For example, studies have contrasted longer and shorter custodial sentences, different forms of custodial sentence, custodial sentences with non-custodial sentences and different forms of non-custodial sentence. In addition studies have sought to examine the effect of introducing, or making more intense, various forms of therapeutic or reformative procedure. Reviews of this literature (eg Bailey, 1966; Lipton et al, 1975; Brody, 1976; Rutter and Giller, 1983) have generally concluded that no type of sentence or form of treatment has been shown to be consistently superior to any other in its impact on reconviction. Taken in conjunction with findings indicating that the rate of offending is dependent upon offenders' previous criminal history and upon their current living situation[1],

---

[1] eg quality of family relationships whilst living at home; quality of the institutional environment whilst in an institution.

this has led to considerable scepticism about the likely outcome of experiments which involve different types of custodial regime (Sinclair and Clarke, 1982). Essentially it is argued that although experimental regimes may sometimes affect the way inmates behave, this effect is limited to the period when the regime itself forms a part of the inmate's current circumstances; unless the situation to which inmates return on release has been improved, there is no reason to expect any substantial reduction in reconviction rates.

6.3 It is not clear whether this general scepticism should be extended to the pilot project. No doubt the possible long term effects of custodial regimes are limited by the influence of the environment into which offenders are released, but the extent of this limitation is not clear. Documented effects of an offender's circumstances on the probability of reconviction are themselves not large enough to rule out the possibility of custodial regimes having a long term (ie post-release) influence on offending. Moreover, previously explored variations in custodial regimes bear little resemblance to that proposed by the Note of Guidance for the pilot regimes. Thus we cannot conclude that the effects produced by the pilot regimes are bound to be as limited as those resulting from previous experiments. Nevertheless, in the light of previous experience, it is reasonable to suppose that any advantage the pilot regimes have over ordinary regimes may be relatively small.

6.4 Assessing whether introducing an experimental regime has had a small effect on reconviction rates poses problems which would not arise if the anticipated effect were a larger one. The basic difficulty is that a small difference in observed reconviction rates could arise in a number of ways unrelated to the effect of the pilot regime

itself. These include: sampling error; biased
samples (ie some samples being more risky, perhaps
having a worse criminal history); changes in the
regimes or the catchment areas on which the
centres draw which are accidentally correlated
with the introduction of the pilot regime (eg a
change in police practice in a particular
catchment area); and incidental consequences of
the introduction of the new regimes (eg a change
in the behaviour of supervising officers
consequent upon their knowledge that a trainee has
been discharged from the 'tough' regime). The
degree to which these effects may be minimised by
aspects of experimental design or statistical
analysis varies. Details will be given in the
sections headed methodology and discussion.

METHODOLOGY

Data collection

6.5 As described in Chapter 2, information about
trainees' previous and current convictions for
standard list offences was provided by the
Offenders' Index for trainees received into the
two pilot and four comparison centres during
period I and period II.

6.6 The Offenders' Index also provided
reconviction data which enabled us to discover
whether or not each trainee had been reconvicted
during the twelve months following release (see
Note 6.1 at the end of this chapter for a
discussion of the follow-up period).

Data analysis

6.7 Reconviction rates were calculated for both
periods at each centre. Senior and junior data
were analysed separately. For the senior data
method B (described in Note 2.2 to Chapter 2) was
used to deal with changes in catchment area.

6.8 The various groups being compared differed somewhat in respect of age distribution at entry and variables measuring criminal history. Because it is known that the probability of reconviction is related both to age and criminal history, it is desirable to allow for differences in these properties. This is done by a process sometimes called internal standardisation. Essentially one establishes from the data the relation between reconviction rate and, say, age and then uses that relation to adjust the separate reconviction rates at the different centres and periods to a common reference level for, say, mean age. This process is done entirely separately for senior and junior centres.

6.9 The reconviction rates in Tables 6.2 and 6.3 are adjusted in this way. Thus differences between them cannot be accounted for by differences between periods or centres in age distribution or criminal history, as measured here (see Note 6.3 for a full list of trainee characteristics allowed for in this way).

6.10 There are a number of variants in the method of standardisation, notably concerning the precise form of relation fitted, and as to whether adjustment is with respect to a relatively large or a relatively small set of variables. It has been checked that the conclusions do not depend upon the precise method used. Some further, more technical, details are given in Note 6.2 at the end of this chapter.

6.11 As well as showing reconviction rates, Tables 6.2 and 6.3 give two additional quantities to aid interpretation. 'Estimated effect of regime change' shows the degree to which the results for the pilot regime deviate from those which would have been expected to occur in the experimental centre had the pilot regime not been introduced.

A different (but logically equivalent) way of describing this quantity is to say that it contrasts the difference between period I and period II results for Send or New Hall (where the pilot regime was introduced) to the difference between period I and II results for the relevant comparison centres (where the regimes had not been deliberately modified)[2]. 'Significance' is the probability of the occurrence of an 'estimated effect of regime change' at least as large as that observed if there was no real effect of regime (ie if there was really no difference between pilot and ordinary regimes).

RESULTS

Junior centres

6.12 Table 6.1 shows the reconviction rates for the junior centres. Two features of these figures are noteworthy. The period I reconviction rate for Send is almost identical to the period II reconviction rate: the introduction of the pilot regime seems to have had no discernible effect. The reconviction rates for the comparison centres also did not seem to vary between period I and period II. We estimate that the reconviction rate observed for Send during period II (when the pilot regime was in operation) is very slightly lower (1.3%) than might have been expected if the pilot regime had not been introduced. This difference is, however, well within the margin of error of the statistical techniques involved: it is small

---

[2] In calculating this quantity, results are averaged across the two relevant comparison centres, giving more weight to the comparison centre with the larger samples. See Note 5.4 to Chapter 5 for a more extended account of the meaning of this quantity.

TABLE 6.1 Reconviction rates for junior centres

Detention centre	Send		Eastwood Park	
Period	I	II	I	II
Type of regime	Ordinary	Pilot	Ordinary	Ordinary
% Reconvicted in 12 months follow up	57%	57%	50%	51%

TABLE 6.2 Reconviction rates for senior centres

Detention centre	New Hall		Buckley Hall	
Period	I	II	I	II
Type of regime	Ordinary	Pilot	Ordinary	Ordinary
% Reconvicted in 12 months follow up	46%	48%	48%	52%

Campsfield House		Estimated effect of regime change	Statistical significance
I Ordinary	II Ordinary		
50%	51%	-1.3%	Not significant

Werrington House		Estimated effect of regime change	Statistical significance
I Ordinary	II Ordinary		
47%	43%	+1.6%	Not significant

enough to be attributable to chance. A second
feature of the results for the junior centres is
that the reconviction rates for Send are
consistently a little higher than those for
Eastwood Park or Campsfield House. This
difference is, however, only marginally
statistically reliable[3].

Senior centres

6.13 Table 6.2 shows the reconviction rates for
the senior centres. Again, the period I
reconviction rates are very similar to the period
II reconviction rates. The reconviction rate for
the pilot project regime at New Hall is very
slightly (1.6%) higher than might have been
expected for New Hall in period II had the pilot
regime not been introduced. This difference is
well within the margin of error of the statistical
techniques involved: it is small enough to be
attributable to chance.

6.14 An interesting feature of the results for the
senior centres is that trainees sentenced from
that block of Manchester courts transferred from
Buckley Hall's catchment area (period I) to New
Hall's catchment area (period II) had a higher
than expected reconviction rate regardless of the
centre in which they served their sentence. This
effect, which is statistically reliable, has, of
course, been adjusted for in producing the figures
in Table 6.2 (it would otherwise have inflated
both the New Hall period II rate and the Buckley
Hall period I rate).

---

[3] The probability of its arising by chance being less
than 0.1.

218

DISCUSSION

6.15 On the basis of these results, it would seem
that the pilot project regimes had about the same
effect on overall reconviction rates as ordinary
detention centre regimes. Before accepting this
conclusion, however, it is necessary to examine
the possibility that the effect of some other
factor(s) may have masked a distinctive effect of
the pilot regimes on overall reconviction rates.
We have identified four such factors. In the case
of two of these we were able to take steps to
diminish the extent to which they could bias the
results.

6.16 The first of these factors is differences
among the samples in the kinds of trainee
received. We used statistical techniques to
equate the samples on their criminal records but
it is possible that there were differences between
the samples on unmeasured variables. For example,
we did not have personality data for the period I
samples and so were unable to equate the samples
on these variables. A trainee's criminal record
is, however, far and away the most important known
correlate of reconviction in young offenders
(Simon, 1971). Sample bias in unmeasured trainee
characteristics is likely, therefore, to have
distorted the results only to a trivial degree.

6.17 The second of these factors was the change in
the senior detention centres' catchment areas.
The procedures used to reduce the effect of these
changes have limitations. However, the most
obvious way in which the method might have failed
(its failure to take account of the effects of
catchment area changes on regional rivalries)
appears not to have applied (see the discussion in
Note 2.1 to Chapter 2). Moreover, a potential
masking factor which can only have applied to the
senior trainees cannot be used to explain away the

failure of both the pilot regimes to show a distinctive effect on overall reconviction rates.

6.18 In the case of two other potential masking factors, although we have not been able to reduce their effects we were able to obtain information as to the likely seriousness of the distortion that might be created by them.

6.19 The first of these factors is the behaviour of supervising officers. Trainees discharged from detention centres undergo a period of compulsory supervision. If the supervisors' behaviour was affected by a knowledge of the type of regime from which the trainee had been discharged, then this could distort the results. The Probation Inspectorate carried out its own investigation into the supervision experience of a sub-sample of the trainees included in the evaluation research and supervised by the probation service. They have indicated to us that supervisors' behaviour was not much affected by the type of regime from which the trainee was discharged (see Note 6.4 at the end of the chapter).

6.20 The second factor is the general propensity to conviction of young males in the centres' respective catchment areas. This propensity will be influenced by (amongst other things) the behaviour of the police and the behaviour of the courts. Presumably the liability of discharged trainees to be convicted might also be affected by any factors which influenced the general propensity to conviction. Data provided from courts' proceedings statistics (and presented in Chapter 7) suggest, however, that the general propensity of young males to conviction did not change in a way which could have distorted the reconviction results.

6.21 To sum up then, our results suggest that the pilot regimes do not have a distinctive effect on overall reconviction rates. We identified four factors which might potentially have distorted these results but none of them seems likely to have caused more than a trivial degree of distortion. It seems reasonable, therefore, to conclude that the pilot project regimes had about the same effect on overall reconviction rates as ordinary detention centre regimes.

6.22 Apart from the main result, there are two subsidiary findings that require discussion. The first is the tendency of Send trainees to be reconvicted at a slightly higher rate than trainees sent to the other junior centres. Not too much should be made of this since the result was only marginally statistically reliable. However, Send trainees also tended to misbehave more whilst in detention centre (as indicated by self-reported deviance and loss of remission), so the result is compatible with Sinclair and Clarke's (1982) hypothesis that delinquent responses established in an institution may generalise to a limited extent to the outside world. It is important to note that these results, both for reconviction and institutional misbehaviour, were more or less the same in both periods. Thus they have nothing to do with the pilot regime as such, being instead a consistent feature of Send. There is, of course, another possible explanation for the higher reconviction rate of Send trainees. The three centres have different catchment areas. It is possible that Send's essentially London catchment area may have been more conducive to offending than the Eastwood Park or Campsfield catchment areas.

6.23 The plausibility of this latter interpretation is increased by the second subsidiary finding: the tendency of trainees sentenced by Manchester courts to be reconvicted more often than other Buckley Hall or New Hall trainees. The Manchester trainees have a higher average number of previous convictions as well. This, however, is not the explanation for their higher reconviction rate since the difference in reconviction rates remains even when the groups are equated statistically on number of previous convictions (and other criminal history variables). These results would occur either if the Manchester environment was conducive to offending or if offences there more commonly resulted in convictions.

NOTES TO CHAPTER 6

Note 6.1 Follow up period

6.24 The use of a twelve month follow up period in place of the more usual twenty four month follow up requires some explanation. The reason for our using the shorter follow up period was a concern not to delay the evaluation report for a further year. Use of the shorter follow up has one additional advantage and two disadvantages. The additional advantage is a statistical one: one-year reconviction rates for both junior and senior trainees tend to be relatively close to 50% whereas two-year reconviction rates are close to 50% only for senior trainees. The relevance of this is that statistical significance testing procedures are more powerful for dichotomous dependent variables with an even split than they are for dichotomous variables with a more extreme split. The most obvious disadvantage is that some of those trainees who are counted as 'not reconvicted' with a twelve month follow up will eventually be reconvicted. Even so the majority of offences do not result in convictions, and it is reasonable to suppose that the probability of being reconvicted within a specified period is influenced by the frequency and seriousness of the offences committed during that period[4]. One year reconviction rates can, therefore, be taken as an indicator of the extent of reoffending. The second disadvantage of using a twelve month follow up is that it makes it difficult to examine

---

[4] Seriousness influences both the probability of an offence being reported to the police (Hough and Mayhew, 1983) and the clear up rate once an offence has been reported. Frequency of offending must increase the probability of reconviction so long as the correlation between frequency of offending and the average risk (per offence) of being caught is not negative.

reconviction for offences, such as offences against the person, which are relatively infrequently committed by detention centre trainees and hence are too rare to make a statistical analysis feasible.

Note 6.2 The statistical analysis

6.25 The basic procedure used in analysing reconviction rates was an analysis of covariance. Period and centre were treated as factors and criminal history variables were entered as covariates (see Note 6.3). The analysis was implemented using the General Linear Model program from the SAS package (SAS Institute, 1982). The ESTIMATE option was used to partition the period by centre interaction effect so as to yield the quantity called 'estimated effect of regime change' in the text. The LSMEANS option was used to produce the adjusted reconviction rates shown in Tables 6.1 and 6.2.

6.26 A number of variants of this basic procedure have been explored to determine the degree to which the results obtained depend upon the exact forms of the analysis. These include:-

i.   Use of logistic regression in place of ordinary least squares to fit the models. The rationale for this variant was that logistic regression is more appropriate for a dichotomous dependent variable than is the ordinary least squares procedure. In practice, however, as would be expected on theoretical grounds in this instance the two methods of fitting models gave virtually identical results.

ii.   Use of a limited set of covariates rather than the full set. Only a few of the covariates actually made much contribution to predicting reconviction. Analyses were

repeated using only those, more important,
covariates in the hope that this might
sharpen significance levels. In fact, only
the most trivial change occurred.

iii. Use of non-parallel covariates. Analysis of
covariance assumes that the covariates
relationship to the dependent variable is the
same in each of the groups being compared.
More complex models, involving interactions
between covariates and factors, can however,
be specified. These have been used to test
this parallelism of covariates assumption.
In a few instances the assumption was
violated. Specifically, the relationship
between reconviction rate and a record of
violent offending varied between groups to a
statistically significant degree in both
senior and junior data sets. However,
dividing the samples on the basis of violent
offences and repeating the main analysis did
not identify a statistically reliable effect
of introducing the pilot regimes in either
sub-sample. Interestingly, further
interactions were found between trainee
characteristics and centre for the
personality data available on period II
cases: Send trainees of below average
intelligence and low psychoticism appeared to
be reconvicted less often than would have
been expected on the basis of experience at
other establishments. Such interactions have
often proved difficult to replicate, however,
so it seemed sensible not to pursue this line
of analysis in the absence of further
reconvictions data.

iv. Use of method A in place of method B to allow
for catchment area changes in the senior
centres. The alternative methods of allowing
for catchment area changes are described in
Note 2.2 at the end of chapter two. In fact,
method A gave very similar results to those
obtained with method B.

Note 6.3 A list of covariates

6.27 The set of covariates used here is less comprehensive than that used for the analyses reported in Chapter 5. This is because those analyses were based on the occupation samples for which additional information was gathered by interviewing trainees.

1.   Number of previous convictions: the number of separate occasions on which the trainee had previously been convicted. It should be noted that he might have been convicted for more than one offence on each occasion. This variable is coded into eight categories, zero through six, and seven or higher (coded as seven).

2.   Conviction volume: seven offence categories are distinguished (violence, sex offences, burglary, robbery, theft, fraud and criminal damage). For each offence category separately, the number of occasions on which the trainee was convicted for an offence in that category is counted. These counts are then added together to give the 'conviction volume' variable.

3.   Duration: the trainee's age on sentence minus the trainee's age on first conviction. Coded in years.

4.   Age on sentence: coded in years

5.   Supervision experience: ever been subject to either a probation order or a supervision order (coded 1 = yes, 0 = no)

6.   Previous detention centre: ever served a detention centre sentence before (coded 1 = yes, 0 = no)

7.   Summary violence: any summary convictions for violence (coded 1 = yes, 0 = no)

8. Violence: any violence convictions except summary convictions (coded 1 = yes, 0 = no)

9. Robbery: any robbery convictions (coded 1 = yes, 0 = no)

10. Burglary: any burglary convictions (coded 1 = yes, 0 = no)

11. Theft: any theft convictions (coded 1 = yes, 0 = no)

12. Fraud: any fraud convictions (coded 1 = yes, 0 = no)

13. Criminal damage: any criminal damage convictions (coded 1 = yes, 0 = no)

Note 6.4 The Probation Inspectorate's investigation into the supervision of trainees from the pilot project regimes

6.28 As part of its normal activity in monitoring the work of the probation service the Probation Inspectorate of the Home Office paid particular attention to work of the service with offenders entering detention centres during the first year of the operation of the tougher regimes. The Criminal Justice Act 1982 had not then been brought into force and supervision lasted for 12 months.

6.29 Probation officers may be involved with detention centre trainees at a number of possible stages: when preparing reports to assist the courts at the sentencing stage; during the sentence when they may be involved with the trainee and his family in preparation for release; and following release when the trainee is under statutory supervision in the community.

6.30 There was evidence of concern among some probation officers about possibly damaging effects of the toughened regimes on trainees during the custody phase of the sentence. This concern resulted in closer contact between probation officers and institutions in a number of cases and possibly in more immediate and concerted action by the Prison Department and probation staff in dealing with trainees showing signs of maladjustment or emotional problems. There was no evidence, however, that probation officers writing social inquiry reports before sentence made any distinction between toughened or non-toughened regimes.

6.31 In some areas probation officers' contacts with trainees from tougher regimes were marginally more frequent in the first month or two after release, but no differences were apparent in the content of interviews or the focus of work. Within two or three months of release no differences were discernible in the handling of cases from toughened or non-toughened regimes. There was a common finding that trainees from toughened regimes, particularly juveniles, 'opened up' and responded in a more lively way during and immediately after their period in custody but this, like most other effects, appeared to wear off within about three months of trainees returning to their home areas.

7. GENERAL DETERRENCE AND EFFECTS ON SENTENCING PRACTICE

7.1 The chapters so far have concentrated on the pilot project regimes and effects they have had on the trainees actually committed to them. This chapter, however, considers whether there might have been more general effects. Data routinely collected by the Home Office Statistical Department have been examined to discover any evidence that the rate at which offences are committed was affected by either the announcement or the implementation of the pilot project regimes. The question whether the courts had been influenced in their sentencing has also been considered. No special study was commissioned, outside the establishments concerned, to discover directly from people in the community at large whether, for example, young people were aware of the pilot project.

Effects on offending

7.2 The announcement and implementation of the pilot project regimes might have influenced offending in a number of ways. The most obvious of these is general deterrence. Young men living within the vicinity of Send and New Hall may have been deterred from offending by the prospect of receiving a sentence which would expose them to the new 'tough' regime. In addition to this localised deterrent effect, national effects might have occurred. The publicity attending the announcement and implementation of the new regimes might have heightened public awareness of custodial penalties, thereby enhancing their general deterrent effect throughout the country. Apart from deterrence there are other effects which could have operated upon a national scale (see Gibbs, 1975 for examples).

7.3 These possibilities suggest that a reduction
in the crime rate might be observed following
either the announcement or the implementation of
the pilot project. In addition such a reduction
might be concentrated in the catchment areas of
Send and New Hall.

7.4 There are however certain difficulties in
detecting any such effects. Previous research
suggests that there is little relationship between
crime rates and the average severity of custodial
sentences (Beylefeld, 1978). It seems reasonable
to infer from this that any effects would most
probably be small. Consequently they might easily
be masked by fluctuations in the crime rate
resulting from other influences. Our ability to
detect possible effects on the crime rate is
further limited by the quality of the available
information. For example, levels of reported
crime do not fully reflect the amount of crime
committed, and changes in the former need not
necessarily correspond to changes in the latter.
Moreover, using figures for the amount of reported
crime does not enable one to know to what extent a
particular age group is committing these crimes.
If, in order to attempt to overcome this problem,
the figures are examined for those actually
convicted, (which enables one to know the age of
the offenders), a different point arises since
those convicted represent only a proportion of
those who offended; changes in the numbers of
those convicted will not necessarily reflect
changes in the real numbers of those offending.
Again, any particular deterrent effect of the
announcement or implementation of the pilot
project could not easily be separated from
possible wider deterrent factors such as the
enunciation by the government of a tougher
approach generally to law and order. These are
but a few of the methodological hazards in this
area. Therefore, our ability to detect effects is
likely to be very restricted.

7.5 Despite these difficulties statistics of offences known to the police have been examined for both some northern police forces (to compare with New Hall) and some southern police forces (to compare with Send)[1]. Total recorded crime figures have been examined as well as figures for burglary (chosen both because substantial numbers of detention centre trainees are convicted of burglary and because statistics of burglary were largely unaffected by changes in counting rules from the start of 1980). All these figures have been related to the population of the area.

7.6 It is clear from the statistical examination of these data that if there had been a general effect on the levels of crime at or soon after the stage when the tougher regime pilot project was being announced and implemented, then it has not been possible to distinguish this effect from the general movement in levels of recorded crime.

7.7 Turning to the extent to which young males have been sentenced, Figure 7.1 shows numbers of convictions in the courts for England and Wales and for the two catchment areas for New Hall (ages 17-20) and Send (ages 14-16). Again any effect that the pilot project might have had, either locally or nationally, is not discernible from these data.

---

[1] The statistics referred to are not contained in this report but can be obtained from the Home Office Statistical Department, Room 839, Queen Anne's Gate, SW1. The northern police forces examined were Derbyshire, Greater Manchester, Lancashire, North Yorkshire, South Yorkshire and West Yorkshire. The southern police forces examined were Surrey, the Metropolitan Police district, Kent, Sussex, Thames Valley and Hampshire.

Figure 7.1 Boys sentenced: 1978—1982 All Offences

a) Boys aged 14 and under 17 sentenced at magistrates cou...

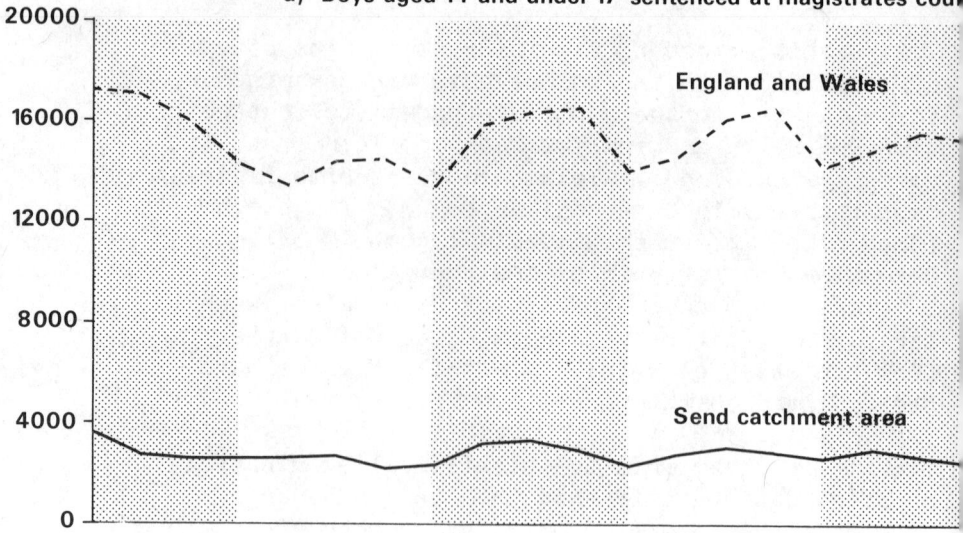

England and Wales

Send catchment area

b) Boys aged 17 and under 21 sentenced at Crown Courts

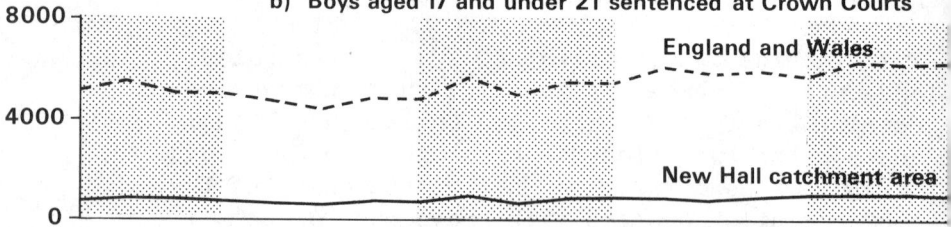

England and Wales

New Hall catchment area

c) Boys aged 17 and under 21 sentenced at magistrates court

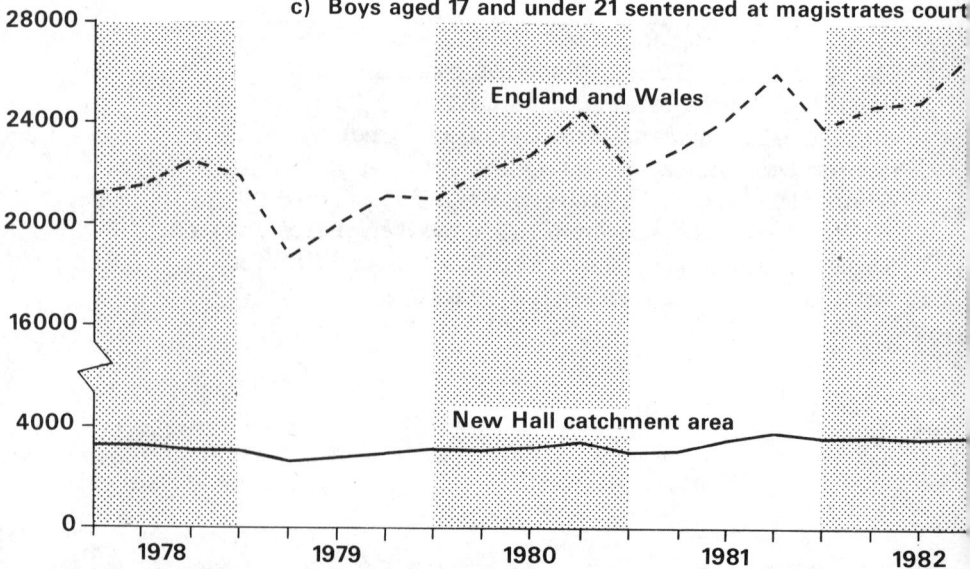

England and Wales

New Hall catchment area

1978   1979   1980   1981   1982

232

Sentencing practice

7.8 We have also considered whether there have
been any changes in sentencing practice as a
result of the implementation of the pilot project,
for example, in the extent to which the courts
regarded detention centre as the preferred
sentence for young offenders generally or for
certain kinds of offender.

7.9 Figures 7.2 and 7.3 show the proportionate
use of junior and senior detention centres by the
courts; for all indictable offences for the New
Hall and then Send catchment areas in comparison
with the whole of England and Wales; and for a
number of separate offence groups, substantial
enough to warrant separate analysis. Again there
is no evidence of any important changes in the
proportions of offenders for whom detention centre
orders were made by the courts in the relevant
catchment areas in comparison with the whole of
England and Wales.

7.10 This information, together with that in Table
7.1 (on overall numbers being sentenced to
detention centre), suggests that it is not the
case that two trends have cancelled each other
out; that is, the courts have not simply adjusted
their rate of sentencing to detention centre in
response to different numbers to be sentenced.

7.11 Table 7.1 also shows a split between three
month and six month detention centre orders for
the New Hall catchment area, for the rest of the
country, and for England and Wales for 1978-82,
for the senior age range. It will be noted that
there is a 1979 peak in the proportion of those
who received the longer sentence. This is the
most marked in the catchment area for New Hall
compared with the rest of the country (including
the Manchester area which in 1979 had not yet been

added to the New Hall catchment area). After 1979
the proportion of six months orders falls and it
is no longer possible to distinguish any
difference between the New Hall catchment area and
the rest of the country. Whilst it is conceivable
that this might be attributed to the courts in the
New Hall catchment area concentrating more on
three months sentences in order to utilise the
pilot project regime at New Hall, other
interpretations might be just as plausible,
particularly as the 1979 peak has not been
explained. Junior detention centre sentencing
figures have never included an appreciable number
of six months sentences by comparison with the
seniors and there was no point in examining junior
figures for a similar tendency.

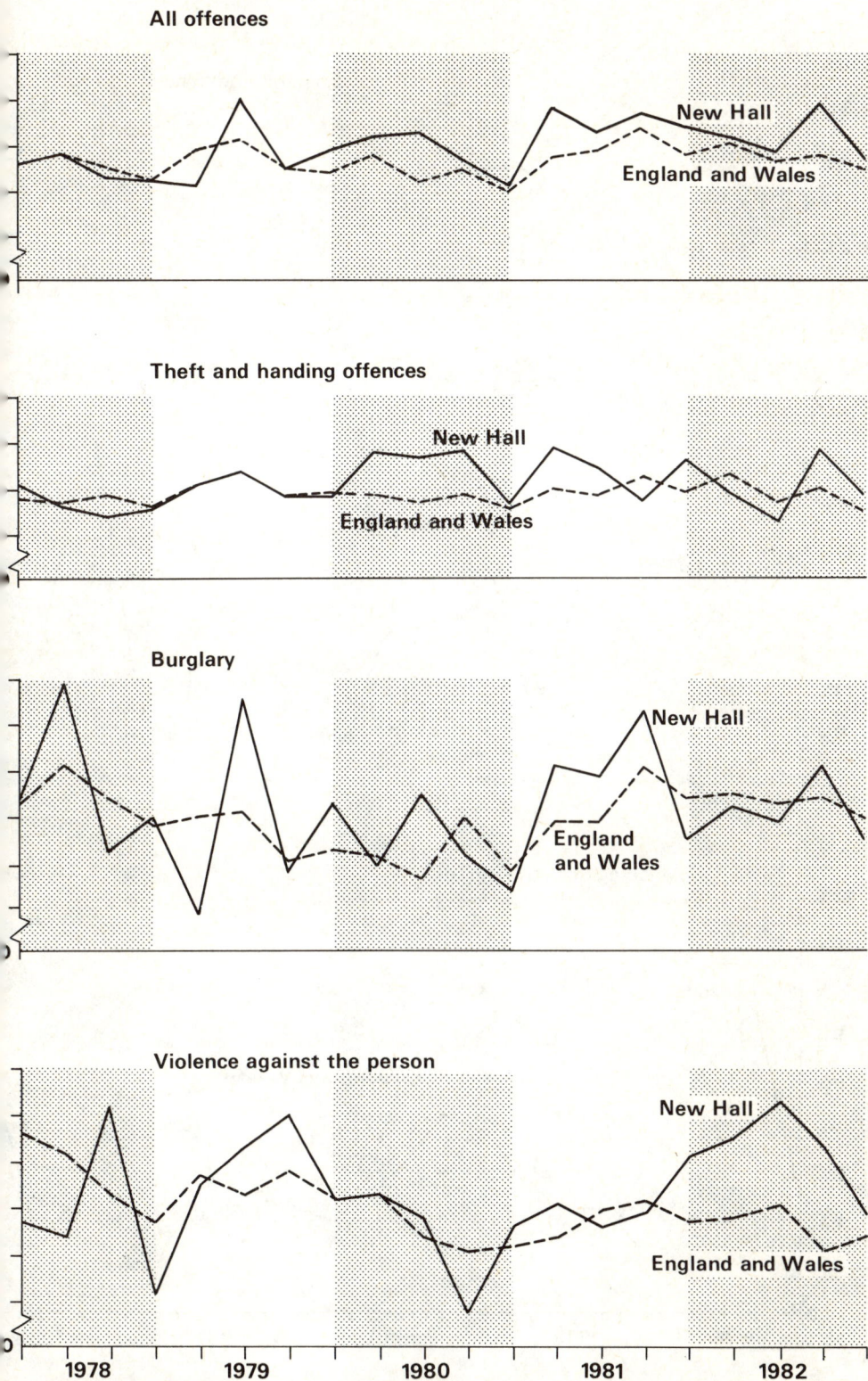

Percentages of Convicted boys aged 17 and under 21 sentenced to Detention Centre

All offences

New Hall

England and Wales

Theft and handing offences

New Hall

England and Wales

Burglary

New Hall

England and Wales

Violence against the person

New Hall

England and Wales

1978   1979   1980   1981   1982

235

Figure 7.3 Percentages of Convicted boys aged 14 and under 17 sentenced to Detention Centre

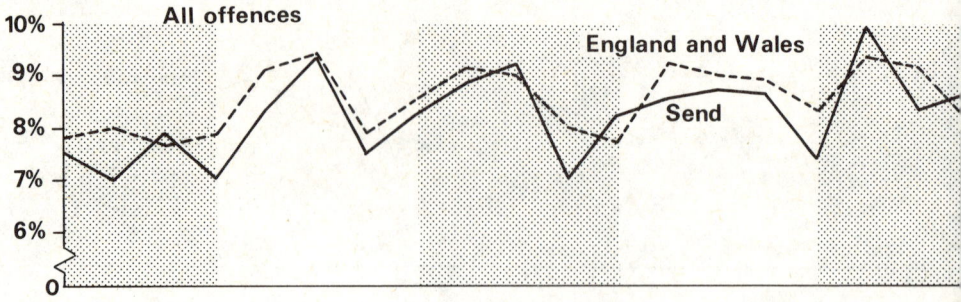

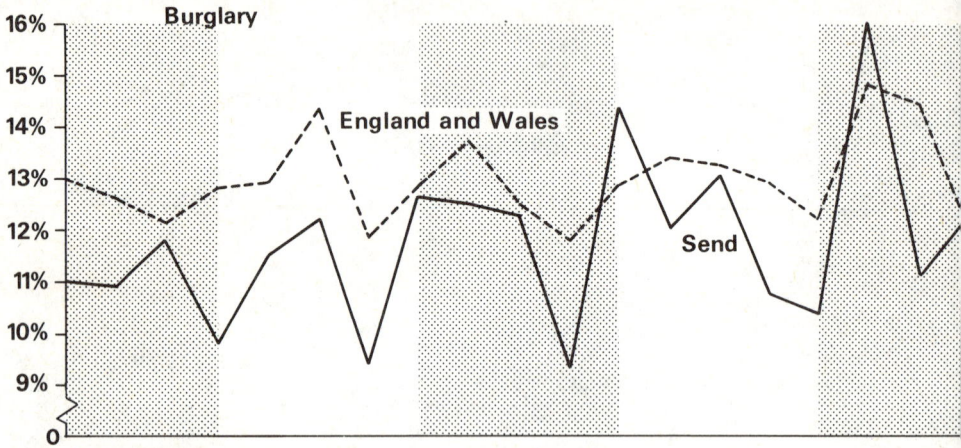

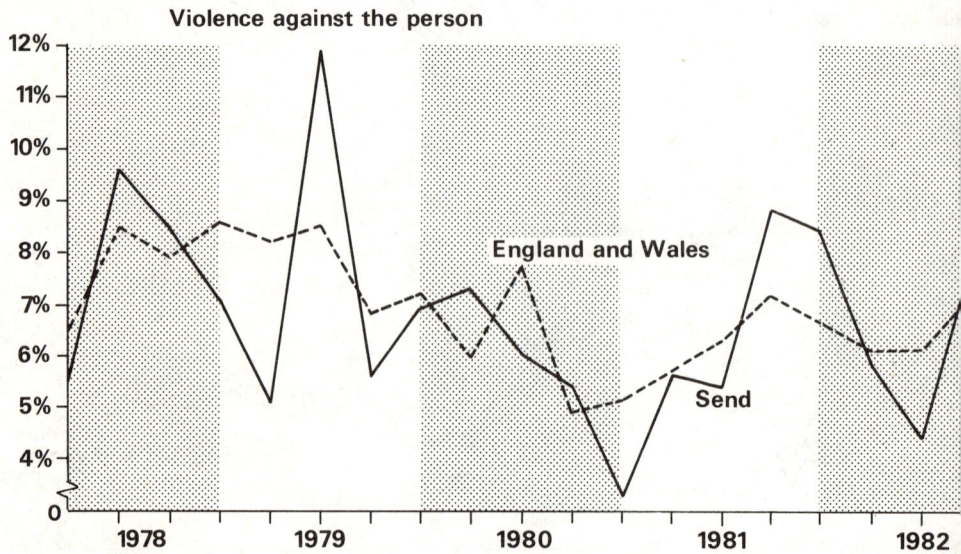

Table 7.1 Males aged 17 and under 21 sentenced to detention centre

	Magistrates' courts				Crown Court				All courts			
	3 mth	6 mth	Total[1]	% 6 mth	3 mth	6 mth	Total[1]	% 6 mth	3 mth	6 mth	Total[1]	% 6 mth
New Hall catchment area												
1978	422	91	513	17.7	264	89	353	25.2	686	180	866	20.8
1979	412	133	545	24.4	194	97	291	33.3	606	230	836	27.5
1980	533	90	623	14.4	230	100	330	30.3	763	190	953	19.9
1981	655	70	725	9.7	326	96	422	22.7	981	168	1147	14.6
1982	642	62	704	8.8	353	80	432	18.5	995	142	1137	12.5
Rest of England & Wales												
1978	2701	483	3184	15.2	1264	452	1716	26.3	3965	935	4900	19.1
1979	2749	495	3244	15.3	1056	405	1461	27.7	3805	900	4705	19.1
1980	2973	431	3404	12.7	1169	452	1621	27.9	4142	883	5034	17.5
1981	3638	416	4054	10.3	1501	395	1896	20.8	5139	809	5950	13.6
1982	3608	330	3938	8.4	1636	464	2100	22.1	5244	794	6038	13.2
England & Wales												
1978	3123	574	3697	15.5	1528	541	2069	26.1	4651	1115	5766	19.3
1979	3161	628	3789	16.6	1250	502	1752	28.6	4411	1130	5541	20.4
1980	3506	521	4027	12.9	1399	552	1951	28.3	4905	1073	5978	17.9
1981	4293	486	4779	10.2	1827	491	2318	21.2	6120	977	7097	13.8
1982	4250	392	4642	8.4	1989	544	2533	21.5	6239	936	7175	13.0

1 Excluding the small number of persons sentenced to other than 3 or 6 months.

8. CONCLUSIONS

8.1 This chapter summarises the findings reported in more detail in earlier chapters.

a. Characteristics of trainees

8.2 One in five of the junior trainees sampled and one in ten of the seniors had not been previously convicted. At the other end of the scale, at least 10% of both groups had been convicted at least seven times and about half of the total number had previously been convicted on three or more occasions. Burglary and theft were the offences most likely to appear in the records, followed by offences concerned with motor vehicles. Those who had been convicted of an offence against the person were in a minority - albeit a sizeable one - just over a quarter of the juniors and about a third of the seniors.

8.3 Under 10% of the trainees had served a previous detention centre sentence. Local authority residential care had, however, been experienced by about half the junior trainees and about a quarter of the senior trainees.

8.4 Personality tests suggest that both junior and senior trainee samples, compared with the normal population of the same age outside, contained a disproportionate number of temperamentally difficult and unhappy individuals. About half of those trainees who had been in local authority residential care reported having absconded at least once, and some (especially amongst the juniors) had absconded repeatedly. Eleven per cent of the juniors and seven per cent of the seniors had a history of self-injury.

238

8.5 The majority of trainees came from families
of intermediate occupational status. They were
probably not different in intelligence from
similar age groups outside. Perhaps 10% were
illiterate. For the senior trainees, the vast
majority of whom had left school, nearly a half
were unemployed prior to detention centre.

b. **The routines**

8.6 Implementing the pilot regimes at Send and
New Hall involved a number of changes in the
routines of these establishments: some activities
were newly introduced, some were elaborated or
emphasised, others were dropped or diminished.

8.7 Extra physical education was introduced,
together with a change in emphasis in the physical
education programme as a whole towards effort
rather than physical skills. Parades and
inspections had been emphasised under the old
regime; these were increased somewhat in number.
Formal drill was introduced and was sustained as
was required. Elements of drill had remained from
much earlier regimes to differing extents in
different centres but these vestiges were clearly
replaced by formal and defined drill sessions (in
accordance with a drill manual) within the
timetable.

8.8 For most of the trainees at Send most of the
time required for the increased physical education
programme came out of that previously allocated to
daytime education classes. At both establishments
only those education classes thought to be
compatible with the new regime were retained. At
New Hall the time required for drill and extra
physical education came out of that previously
allocated to work, and the continuity of work was
broken up (this was partly remedied by timetable
changes implemented in September 1980).

8.9   There were also changes in the content and organisation of the work programme designed to make it more strenuous. Thus there were some adjustments in the size and supervision of work parties, numbers in such relatively less demanding jobs as orderlies were limited, a workshop at Send and a construction course at New Hall were closed, and numbers assigned to market gardening at Send and to farming and weaving at New Hall were increased.

c.   **Implementation by staff**

8.10 Routines attain their quality, at least in part, from the way in which staff impose them. Experience of the pilot project has shown considerable variation in the extent to which staff have been able to increase the demands experienced by the trainees.

8.11 In standards of cleanliness, and other features regularly inspected, there seems to have been considerable effort to maintain and even improve standards, but there was little room for improvement over previously high standards.

8.12 In physical education the change in content and the extra time may have imposed more strenuous demands upon the trainees, but the extent to which this occurred was limited both by injunctions within the Note of Guidance and by the accepted philosophy and standards for physical education which preclude administering it in a punitive way.

8.13 Drill and parades were not intended to be demoralising or punitive and staff showed considerable patience and willingness to demonstrate or repeatedly explain manoeuvres that the trainees found difficult, though they were swift to clamp down on apparent lack of effort.

8.14 Drill entailed staff requiring prompt and co-ordinated responses to a string of instructions. This probably put trainees under more pressure, at least during the first fortnight while the drill was still being mastered, than did those education classes which were lost in the new timetable at Send. At New Hall, where drill and extra physical education replaced work, the matter is less clear cut. Sustained work imposes a different kind of demand but not necessarily one which is easier to meet. Rather the main contrast is between the active 'instructor' stance of staff drilling trainees as opposed to the passive, supervisory stance commonly entailed in keeping trainees working.

8.15 Finally, there is evidence that the introduction of the pilot regimes led to an increased use of formal punishment. This increase was statistically reliable only at Send, being weaker at New Hall. It may have resulted from Send staff being somewhat stricter in relation to minor infractions.

d.   **Trainees' experience of the regime**

8.16 There were differences between the junior and senior centres in the ways in which the trainees experienced the pilot regimes.

8.17 In both centres the trainees who had experienced the pilot regime appeared to look upon staff more positively, seeing them as fairer, easier to trust, and more concerned about trainees, than did trainees in the year preceding the pilot project. This effect was more marked, however, at New Hall than it was at Send.

8.18 In addition, at New Hall alone, the amount of stress experienced by trainees declined and the proportion of trainees describing themselves as

having an easy time rose after the introduction of
the pilot regime. Trainees' accounts of their own
experiences is confirmed by staff, who also
considered that the regime at New Hall had become
easier for trainees. Many staff there were
convinced that the virtues of hard, continuous if
monotonous work were preferable to the varied
programme which the regular drill and extra
physical education required. At both
establishments the observers too noted that drill
soon became an enjoyable pursuit. A separate
investigation of trainee attitudes to the various
components of their detention centre life showed
that the items which they were least likely to
like were the mundane work tasks with an element
of dirt or drudgery about them; the drill was by
comparison popular and aspects of physical
education positively attractive.

8.19 Thus the pilot regime at New Hall may have
been easier and less stressful because the time
for drill and physical education was taken out of
that allocated for work. The absence of change at
Send in these aspects of trainee experience may
reflect the fact that there it was the time
allocated to daytime education which was reduced
when the timetable was changed.

e.   **Trainee conduct within detention centre**

8.20 Introduction of the pilot regimes seems to
have had comparatively little effect on trainees'
conduct within detention centre. Indices of
bullying, theft, and delinquent activities
generally all suggested that trainees may have
been very slightly better behaved under the pilot
regimes. Not all of these trends were
statistically reliable, however, so they should
not be trusted in the absence of replication.

f.   Reconvictions

8.21 The introduction of the pilot project regimes
had no discernible effect on the rate at which
trainees were reconvicted. A number of ways in
which effects on reconviction might have been
masked were considered and discounted.

g.   Crime rates and sentencing practice

8.22 Investigations of crime rates were limited to
the scrutiny of information which is regularly
collected by the Home Office Statistical
Department. No large effects were discernible.
If there were smaller effects, the data were not
capable of revealing them. Apparently, the
announcement of the policy did not affect crime
rates generally: there was no interruption of
trends in crime among young people generally nor
in the catchment areas of the two pilot project
regimes especially.

8.23 The courts do not seem to have adopted any
systematic different sentencing practice as a
result of the implementation of the regimes -
there was a request that they avoid such changes.

h.   Relationship between trainees' experience and
the effect of the pilot regimes on
reconviction

8.24 The purpose of the pilot project was to
assess whether young offenders can be effectively
deterred from committing further offences by
spending a period of weeks in a detention centre
with a more rigorous and demanding regime. This
purpose can only be fulfilled if in practice the
pilot regimes were actually 'more rigorous and
demanding' than those which they replaced. The
material summarised in the section on trainees'
·experience earlier in this chapter must raise

considerable doubt as to whether the pilot regimes
were actually experienced by trainees as 'more
rigorous and demanding'. The matter is complex
for there is some evidence that the pilot regimes
were stricter and placed new demands on trainees
(in drill for example). However, especially at
New Hall, these changes do not appear to have
produced a regime whose demands trainees found
more difficult to meet. The finding that the
pilot project regimes had about the same effect on
reconviction rates as ordinary detention centre
regimes has to be seen against that background.

NOTES TO CHAPTER 8

Note 8.1 The scope of the report: qualifications

a.   **Establishment/regime interactions**

8.25 The form that any basic type of regime takes
may depend upon the particular features of the
establishment within which it is implemented. The
present report gives some indication of the
possible scale of these variations for ordinary
regimes. Data collected during period I give us
six examples of establishments then running
ordinary regimes. Two of these regimes
(Campsfield House and New Hall) produced a very
different (harder) experience for trainees from
the others.

8.26 Period II data give us two examples of pilot
project regimes (one at Send, one at New Hall).
The somewhat different results obtained suggest
that the effect of implementing a pilot project
type regime may also depend upon the nature of the
establishment within which it is implemented.
Having only two examples of pilot project regimes
makes it difficult to gauge the degree of
similarity that is to be expected between pilot
regimes implemented in different establishments.
(Note 1.2 explains why the new regimes introduced
at Foston Hall and Haslar in September 1981 are
not covered in this report.)

b.   **Fluctuations in the quality of regime**

8.27 Even where the regime prevailing in an
establishment is not deliberately altered, there
may nevertheless be quite substantial fluctuations
in its quality. (The difference between period I
and period II results for Campsfield House gives a
clear example of this.) It would have delayed the
present report too long if we had waited for the
repeated samples needed to assess the degree to
which such fluctuations occurred in the pilot
project regimes.

245

c.   Comparison of the results for different types of offender

8.28 Even where two regimes have about the same effect on reconviction rates it is possible that they have different effects for different types of offender. For example, the kind of treatment that is particularly effective for, say, the intelligent offenders may have deleterious effects for the less intelligent. Such a pattern is called an 'interaction effect'. Effects of this type have been reported sufficiently often for one reviewer (Brody, 1976) to argue that evaluations which do not take account of possible interaction are very much less likely to show positive results.

8.29 To test properly for interaction effect involves subdividing samples into different types of offender and then testing to see whether comparisons between regimes yield reliably different results for those various types. Such tests tend to be quite insensitive unless the original sample size is large. Moreover, where an overall test indicates that a reliable interaction is present, the subsamples into which the data have been divided have to be large enough for it to be possible accurately to identify the types of offender for which treatments have different effects. In addition, the interaction effects reported in the literature have not proved easy to replicate (eg the attempts of Folkard et al (1976) and Fowles (1978) to repeat Shaw's (1974) finding that introverted prisoners were more susceptible to casework by probation officers).

8.30 Whatever the explanation for the fragility of many interaction effects it is clear that this makes them of little practical value. It would only be where an interaction had been demonstrated in repeated samples that it would be of practical use. In the light of these considerations the present samples were deemed too small and too few

246

in number to provide a satisfactory test for
interaction effects.

d.   **Reconviction for violent offences**

8.31 Given the present sample size, the small
number of reconvictions for violent offences in a
one year follow up makes it impossible, in the
present report, to assess on a statistically
meaningful basis the relative impact of different
regimes on the rate at which discharged trainees
are reconvicted for violent offences.

APPENDIX A

TOUGHER REGIMES PILOT PROJECT IN TWO DETENTION
CENTRES

NOTE OF GUIDANCE TO STAFF

Purpose and form of project

A.1 The tougher regimes pilot project will
commence at New Hall senior detention centre and
Send junior detention centre on 21 April 1980.
The purpose of the project is to assess whether
young offenders can be effectively deterred from
committing further offences by spending a period
of weeks in a detention centre with a more
rigorous and demanding regime. The possibility of
introducing shorter detention centre sentences is
under review, but the pilot project will commence
under existing legislation. Therefore the minimum
period in custody, ie assuming full remission of
one half of the sentence for offenders aged 14 and
under 17 and one third of the sentence for those
aged 17 and under 21, will as at present be one
and a half months for those under 17 and two
months for those aged 17 and under 21.

A.2 The project will operate within the framework
of the existing detention centre system. Subject
to the availability of places, all offenders in
the appropriate age groups who receive detention
centre sentences in the two centres' committal
areas will go through the more rigorous regime,
except those who receive more than the three
months' minimum sentence and those who are
physically or mentally unfit for the regime: see
paragraphs A.3 to A.5 below. Subject to what is
said in paragraph A.5, offenders who have been
released from New Hall and Send but are recalled
to custody during their period of supervision will
be returned there.

248

Offenders excluded from the pilot project

A.3 **Offenders sentenced to more than three months.** Offenders who are otherwise eligible for the pilot project by virtue of age and geography, but are sentenced to more than three months (the maximum detention centre sentence is six months) will be excluded from the pilot project through revision of the catchment areas. A circular was issued to the courts in February, the effect of which is that from 25 February 1980 courts in the relevant areas have been committing offenders sentenced to three months to New Hall and Send and those sentenced to longer periods to other detention centres. The catchment areas have been adjusted so far as possible to allow for this: New Hall's catchment area now comprises Greater Manchester, South Yorkshire, West Yorkshire and the High Peak district of Derbyshire; and Send's now consists of the City of London, Greater London, Kent, Surrey, East and West Sussex. The catchment areas may need further revision in the light of experience. If a sentence is increased by more than 25% once an offender is at New Hall or Send, eg at a further court appearance or through the issue of a lodged warrant, the offender will be transferred to another centre when he reaches the EDR (earliest date of release, allowing for remission) on his first sentence. An offender whose sentence is so extended could therefore spend up to an additional two weeks (New Hall) or one and a half weeks (Send) under the tougher regime, plus any remission time lost through disciplinary offences.

A.4 **Persons who are physically or mentally unfit for the regime.** Although offenders may be medically examined at or on behalf of a court before sentence, such examinations are not required by statute and their purpose is to ascertain fitness for detention centres generally.

Under the pilot project, therefore, all offenders who go to New Hall and Send will be examined by the centre's medical officer within 24 hours of their reception, as at present, and will not be subject to the centre's normal regime until this has been done; and any person who is considered by him to be unfit for the regime will be transferred to another detention centre. An offender whose unfitness is temporary will, at the discretion of the medical officer, stay at the centre but his activities, eg PE, will be limited to the extent and for the length of time specified by the medical officer. Once an offender has entered the regime all staff will pay regard to his physical and mental condition: if necessary this will be reported to the medical officer, who may if appropriate limit his activities or decide that he should be transferred elsewhere. The note of Guidance sent by the Director of Prison Medical Services to the medical officer is at Annex A.

Transitional arrangements.

A.5 As part of the transitional arrangements, the courts have been advised that offenders sentenced to three months after 21 February 1980 who go to New Hall or Send may complete their sentences under the tougher regime, but that those who are physically or mentally unfit for the regime will be transferred out by the commencement date. Offenders who were sentenced before 25 February to more than three months and who are not due for release by the commencement date will be transferred elsewhere, as will anyone sentenced before 21 February to three months detention who would be received or remain in custody after the commencement date eg through lost remission, recall to custody or having been on bail pending appeal.

The regime

A.6 The regimes in detention centres are already brisk, and the Department is required by statutory Detention Centre Rules to provide full-time education for detention centre inmates of compulsory school age and part-time education for those over that age. Within these limits, the intention is to place greater emphasis on hard and constructive activities, discipline, tidiness, drill, parades and inspections. The regimes are described in more detail in paragraphs 7 to 18 below: there will be variations between the two centres on account of different age groups and facilities. The new timetables, which will come into full effect by two weeks after the commencement date, are summarised at Annexes B and C. As indicated thereon the timetables for the kitchen parties at both centres, the induction party at Send and the farm stock party at New Hall differ in some respects.

Work

A.7 The aim is to ensure that all work is physically hard. At New Hall it will comprise market gardening and upkeep of internal grounds (about 20 inmates - all figures in this paragraph are approximate; the actual numbers will vary according to the population of the centre and the season of the year), maintenance of outside grounds and gardens (10), care of farm stock (8), other farm work (10), hand-loom weaving (16), engineers work party (14), kitchen party (8), cleaners (10), stores (3) and orderlies (5). At Send most inmates, ie those of compulsory school age will, as well as working in either the mornings or afternoons, follow an educational programme including PE (40 at any one time). Work will comprise: market gardening (40 inmates at any one time during the day), kitchen party (10),

orderlies (6), laundry (2), maintenance of outside
gardens (10) and works department party (5). At
both centres during severe weather work out of
doors will be replaced with other activities
including chopping, sawing and bundling of wood.

Education

A.8 At Send, inmates of compulsory school age
will each week receive approximately 24 hours
education, including seven hours PE (see paragraph
A.9 below). Classroom education will take place
on weekdays, partly in the morning or afternoon
(with work, PE and drill sessions occupying the
other part of the day) and partly in the evenings.
It will be based on school curricula and consist
of english, mathematics, biology, geography,
household management, history, technical drawing,
social studies, art and gardening. Where
necessary remedial education will be given. At
both centres, inmates over compulsory school age
will receive part-time education for up to two
hours on four evenings a week. The programme will
be based on practical, social and academic
studies: at New Hall metalwork and woodwork, car
maintenance, first aid, job searching, employment
conditions, remedial education, mathematics,
social skills, parentcraft, environmental studies,
PE, survival cookery, table tennis coaching (for
the socially inadequate) and cookery and milk
production (for the relevant work parties); and at
Send woodwork, first aid, mathematics, survival
skills, english and PE. Inmates over compulsory
school age who are clearly backward will receive
two hours remedial education during the day;
others who are less backward will receive remedial
education in the evenings. As necessary a few
inmates over compulsory school age will spend one
to two hours a day on maintenance education ie
work linked with formal education or training
courses on which they were engaged before

252

sentence, including occasional day release for
particular sessions or to take practical
examinations. Education sessions generally will
be conducted in such a manner as to reflect the
general tone of the establishment. As part of the
education programme Send will continue to operate
two evening training courses in catering and
gardening for inmates engaged in such work within
the centre. The existing construction industry
training course at New Hall will close before the
pilot project starts, and the inmates concerned
with be employed on work parties.

Physical education

A.9 As at present, PE will concentrate on the
development of physical skills and related fitness
training which will be of use to inmates after
release. On average inmates will receive 1 hour
20 minutes PE on each weekday: the amount and
type of PE will vary during the sentence and on
different days. Inmates will receive remedial PE
as necessary.

Religion

A.10 As at present, the Chaplains will organise
voluntary classes or religious worship on one or
two evenings a week, and inmates who belong to a
major religious denomination will be required to
attend a weekly service.

External activities

A.11 External activities will be limited at Send
to occasional public gymnastics displays, and at
New Hall to Sunday community service work in a
local Shaftesbury Home which caters primarily for
muscular dystrophy patients.

Parades and inspections

A.12 Both establishments will hold a series of
parades during the day. Their purpose will be to
check inmate numbers before and after work period,
to reassemble inmates into different parties at
the changeover between activities (work, PE,
drill, education, meals), to facilitate
redeployment of staff between different
activities, to inspect inmates' clothing and
deportment, and to carry out drill (see paragraph
A.13 below). In addition, on weekdays inmates and
their kit will be inspected in dormitories.

Drill

A.13 At New Hall on each weekday inmates will
spend a total of one and a quarter hours on drill,
and inmates at Send one hour and ten minutes. At
both centres drill will take place during parades
and at separate drill sessions. The purpose of
drill will be to contribute to the general tone
and tempo of the centre, to encourage trainees to
develop self-discipline and take a pride in their
appearance and bearing; and to provide an
opportunity to develop teamwork and group
discipline. A note of guidance on drill is at
Annex D. Both centres will have parades and drill
at weekends: see paragraph A.16.

Association

A.14 At New Hall there will be 30 minutes
association on each weekday evening. At Send,
which operates a more structured regime for the
junior trainees, there will as at present be no
weekday association. There will be association
periods on Saturdays and Sundays.

Privileges and the grade system

A.15 The grade system at the centre will be retained. The rate of progress between grades will depend on performance. There will be two grades at New Hall: inmates in the second grade will be able to play table tennis during evening association, and to be employed on work parties outside the perimeter fence of the centre. At Send there will be three grades: inmates in the second grade will be allowed some unescorted movement around the establishment, and in some cases television and table tennis; the third grade (and to a lesser extent the second grade) will offer more responsible employment, a smaller dormitory with greater privacy and limited access to television.

Weekends

A.16 The weekends will as at present be taken up largely by inspections, sporting activities, domestic tasks and family visits together with evening association. The morning programmes will include parades and drill sessions.

Visits

A.17 Families will be able to visit inmates on Wednesday, Saturday and Sunday afternoons at New Hall and on weekdays and Saturday afternoons at Send. This represents one change from present arrangements: to minimise disruption to the routine at New Hall, restriction of weekday visits to Wednesday and introduction of Sunday visits. The introduction of Sunday visiting at Send is under consideration.

Handling of inmates

A.18 Inmates will be expected to carry out tasks briskly, but also with care and attention to detail. A high standard of politeness and tidiness will be required. The aim of staff, who will wear uniform at both centres, will be to be firm but fair. The interest taken by staff in the progress and wellbeing of trainees will be a focal part of the project. The personal officer scheme, under which individual members of staff are responsible in this respect for particular inmates, will continue. A note of guidance on the handling of inmates is at Annex E.

Aftercare

A.19 Arrangements for supervision for up to one year after release by the probation or social services will continue. Each centre will as at present have two probation officers seconded to it full-time to assist contact with those services before inmates are released. As at present, designated supervision officers will be encouraged to make contact with inmates before their release, visiting them at the detention centre where appropriate.

Evaluation

A.20 The evaluation programme, much of which was initiated in autumn 1979 in order to obtain a picture of the detention centre system before the form and location of the pilot project were announced, is based primarily on comparisons between New Hall and Send and four other centres: Buckley Hall and Werrington House senior centres and Campsfield House and Eastwood Park junior centres. The evaluation programme (which is summarised at Annex F) will cover the composition and characteristics of the centres' populations,

description of the regime, an assessment so far as
is possible of the effects on inmates while in
custody and (subject to consultation with the
supervising services) under supervision after
release and as reflected in reconviction rates;
and examination of the patterns of offending and
sentencing practice in the committal areas
concerned.

Staff and training

A.21 An important element of the regime will be
close supervision of inmates, particularly during
work, drill and PE sessions. The existing
discipline staff levels at each centre are being
increased accordingly.

A.22 Briefing programmes are being arranged for
staff before the pilot project commences, and the
Officer Training Schools are arranging training
sessions in drill.

TOUGHER REGIMES PILOT PROJECT IN TWO DETENTION
CENTRES

NOTES OF GUIDANCE TO STAFF

NOTES FOR THE MEDICAL OFFICER

A.23 The reception medical examination will be of
particular importance under the tougher regimes
pilot project. The medical officer will
specifically consider whether young offenders
received from the courts are physically or
mentally unfit for the regime so that, if
necessary, arrangements can be made for transfer
elsewhere. The reception examination should be
conducted within the first 24 hours of the arrival
of the trainee, who will not enter the normal
regime of the centre until this has been done.

A.24 The conclusion as to whether a person is
physically or mentally unfit for the regime is a
matter for the clinical judgement of the doctor
concerned based on an appropriate examination and
a knowledge of the programmes to which the
trainees will be subject. The medical officers
concerned should take steps to familiarise
themselves with the regime.

A.25 The medical officers concerned will have had
the benefit of general discussions with a medical
member of the Directorate of Prison Medical
Services about fitness for the tougher regimes.
If the medical officer requires advice about the
suitability for the regime of any individual
trainees, particularly about psychiatric aspects,
he should consult the senior medical officer at
his supervising establishment (SMO Ashford in the
case of Send and SMO Wakefield in the case of New
Hall, to whom copies of these notes are being
sent).

A.26 It is envisaged that the majority of
decisions to transfer a trainee elsewhere will be
reached following the initial medical examination,
but if at any time during the sentence the medical
officer reaches the conclusion that a trainee has
become unfit for the regime he should be
transferred.

A.27 Transfer will be to Campsfield House
detention centre (from Send) and to Buckley Hall
detention centre (from New Hall) except when a
trainee's condition is such as to warrant location
in an establishment with full-time medical officer
cover. In such a case transfer should be to an
appropriate establishment arranged following
consultations with the supervising senior medical
officer.

A.28 It is open to the medical officer to give
specific advice to the warden or physical
education instructor about the activities of any
trainee who is fit for the regime as a whole, but
whose physical capacity may need careful
development in the first instance.

A.29 All members of staff are being reminded that
any cause for concern about the health, mental or
physical, of any trainee should be brought to the
attention of the hospital staff for the
information of the medical officer.

A.30 Any general enquiries may be directed to
Regional principal medical officers or to the
Medical Directorate at Headquarters.

NOTE OF GUIDANCE TO STAFF

TIMETABLES[1] - NEW HALL CENTRE

Weekdays

06.15	Inmates rise, wash, shave, dress, make up beds, dormitories cleaned and inspected.
07.15	Breakfast.
07.45	Work parties change into work clothes.
08.00	Parade.
08.00	Drill/work/PE according to groups.
09.45	Break.
10.00	Work/PE according to group.
12.00	Parade and Drill.
12.15	Wash and change for dinner.
12.30	Dinner.
12.45	Warden's call-ups, adjudications etc. Social workers' call-ups.
13.15	Work parties change into working clothes.
13.30	Parade.
13.30	Work/PE/drill according to groups.
15.20	Break.
15.30	Work/PE/drill according to groups.
16.30	Parade, wash and change.
16.45	Tea.
17.00	Applications, mail, library.
17.30	Methodist group (Wednesday only).
18.00	Classes/PE. C of E and RC Chaplain's session (Wednesdays only).
19.15	Bathing and showers (Wednesdays only).
19.50	Classes end; make beds, boot and shoe cleaning.
20.20	Supper.
20.40	Association.
21.20	To dormitories.
21.30	Lights out.

[1] Timetables applicable to all inmates except kitchen and farm stock parties, whose hours of work differ with some consequential changes elsewhere in the timetable.

METABLES[1] - NEW HALL CENTRE

Saturdays		Sundays	
.00	Inmates rise, wash, shave, dress, make up up beds, clean dormitories.	07.00	Inmates rise, wash, dress, shave, make up beds, clean dormitories
.00	Breakfast.	08.00	Church (C of E only).
.30	Change into working clothes, prepare for inspection.	08.30	Breakfast.
.00	Drill.	09.15	Warden's parade ground inspection.
.30	Warden's call-ups, grade reports, adjudications etc.	09.30	- 10.00 Drill.
.00	Warden's inspection.	10.00	- 10.15 Drill for Grade Is.
.15	Dinner.	10.45	Kit and bed space inspection.
.30	Visits.	11.30	Association.
.00	Visits continue/games and PE.	12.15	Dinner.
		13.30	Visits.
.45	Showers.	14.00	Visits continue/games and PE.
.30	Tea.		
.15	Prepare for Warden's Sunday Inspection, make beds.	15.45	Showers.
.15	Church (RCs only).	16.30	Tea.
.00	Association/games.	17.15	Clothing maintenance, make beds.
.00	Supper. Association continues.	18.00	Association/ games.
.10	To dormitories.	20.00	Supper. Association continues.
.30	Lights out.	21.10	To dormitories.
		21.30	Lights out.

Timetables applicable to all inmates except kitchen and farm stock parties, whose hours of work differ with some consequential changes elsewhere in the timetable.

NOTE OF GUIDANCE TO STAFF

TIMETABLES[1] - SEND DETENTION CENTRE

Weekdays

06.30 Inmates woken, wash, bed spaces cleaned and inspected.
07.30 Breakfast.
08.00 Parade.
08.00 Work/classes/drill/PE according to group.
10.00 Drill.
10.15 Work/classes/drill/PE according to group.
12.00 Parade and drill.
12.20 Dinner.
13.15 Parade.
13.15 Work/classes/drill/PE according to group.
15.00 Drill.
15.15 Work/classes/drill/PE according to group.
16.15 Parade; then change and inspection.
16.40 Tea.
17.15 Boots/domestic cleaning.
18.00 Classes (Monday to Tuesday)/cleaning, bath, kit change (Friday).
20.00 Assemble in dining hall.
20.15 Supper.
20.35 Wash; clean teeth; change socks and pants.
21.00 Settle in dormitories.
21.30 Lights out.

[1] Timetables applicable to all inmates except those newly arrived, who follow an induction programme for their first few days, and kitchen work party whose hours of work differ, with some consequential changes elsewhere in the timetables.

IMETABLES[1] - SEND DETENTION CENTRE

	Saturdays		Sundays
7.15	Inmates woken; wash, bed spaces cleaned and inspected.	07.15	Inmates woken; wash, clean bed spaces.
8.30	Breakfast.	08.30	Breakfast.
9.00	Parade.	09.00	Domestic cleaning; then prepare for Warden's inspection.
9.00	Work/drill (½ hour drill session, by groups, during this or 10.15 period).	09.30	Church (RC's only).
0.00	Drill.	10.30	- 11.15 Warden's inspection of dormitories A and B/drill for C and D.
0.15	Work/drill (see above).	11.15	- 12.00 Warden's inspection of dormitories C and D/drill for A and B.
1.15	Change for inspection.	12.00	Dinner.
1.30	Warden's inspection parade.	13.30	Games and outdoor sports.
2.00	Dinner.	15.30	Showers.
3.30	Visits/outside games and sports.	16.00	Tea.
		16.30	Quiet reading.
5.30	Showers	17.15	Church (Anglicans only).
6.00	Tea.		
7.00	Letter/writing/quiet reading.	18.15	Association.
		20.15	Supper.
8.00	Association.	20.30	Wash, clean teeth, pants and socks change.
0.15	Supper.		
1.00	Settle in dormitories.	21.00	Settle in dormitories.
1.30	Lights out.	21.30	Lights out.

TOUGHER REGIMES PILOT PROJECT IN TWO DETENTION
CENTRES

NOTE OF GUIDANCE TO STAFF

GUIDANCE NOTES ON DRILL

Purpose

A.31   Under the pilot project drill will form a
distinct element of the programme for all
trainees, taking place during parades and separate
sessions for groups of trainees. Its purpose will
be to contribute to the general tone and tempo of
the centre; to encourage trainees to develop self-
discipline and take a pride in their appearance
and bearing; and to provide an opportunity to
develop team work and group discipline. Some
parades and drill sessions will be combined with
inspections, whose purpose will be to encourage
thoroughness and attention to detail.

General guidelines

A.32.1 No drill session should exceed 1 hour, and
any 30 minute period of continuous drill should be
followed by a 5 minute break.

A.32.2 Drill should take place only as part of the
agreed daily programe of the establishment.

A.32.3 Drill should in no circumstances be used as
a sanction.

A.32.4 There should be no double marching or
excessive periods of marking time.

A.32.5 Records of attendance should be kept as for
other formally organised sessions in the centre's
programme.

A.32.6 Staff should be constantly aware of the disparities amongst inmates in size, co-ordination, physical competence and previous experience of drill; and should make appropriate provision in the content and conduct of the session.

A.32.7 Exaggerated arm swinging should be avoided. Arms should swing no higher than midway between waist and shoulder.

A.32.8 Sufficient space for ease of movement should be allowed between each trainee.

A.32.9 Boots will be worn for drill.

Drill programme

A.33   The drill programme will consist of any or all of the following manoeuvres.

A.33.1 Elementary drill training (for inmates in induction party). Stand easy/at ease; attention from stand at ease; turning at the half (left, right, about turn); marching in quick time; halt; falling in on a marker; marking time; falling out.

A.33.2 Group training. Marching in column of threes/twos; wheeling (left and right); turn on the march (left, right, about turn); close and open march; marching in line (advance, retire); turning on the march (inclining); about turn marking time; changing direction in column of threes; changing direction left/right when in line (halt to halt, halt to move, move to halt).

A.33.3 Simple sequences without command

Note   Each session should comprise:-
        Revision of work
        New material
        Practice

The proportion of time spent on each of these will depend upon performance and progress.

TOUGHER REGIME PILOT PROJECT IN TWO DETENTION
CENTRES

NOTE OF GUIDANCE TO STAFF

GUIDANCE ON THE HANDLING OF INMATES

General

A.34 The pilot project is being established within
existing legislation. The intention is to produce
a regime which is both demanding and constructive,
within a brisk and disciplined routine. The more
demanding elements of existing regimes will be
enhanced, and drill and formal parades will assume
greater importance, being treated as distinct
activities in their own right.

A.35 In order to ensure the success of the project
it is of paramount importance that staff should
themselves take pride in and uphold the prison
service's high professional standards, and set an
irreproachable example. The interest taken by
staff in the progress and well-being of trainees
will be a focal part of the project.

Standards of discipline

A.36 It is expected that these will develop from
the combination of regime and staff example
referred to above. No change is being made in the
rules and procedures governing adjudications; nor
is it expected that there will be a need to
increase the frequency of the use of disciplinary
reports. Trainees will be required to march
simply and smartly from place to place and to
maintain a high standard of cleanliness and

personal appearance. All activities will be
supervised and inspections will be an integral
part of the routine.

A.37 Just as it is important to avoid standards
sliding as time passes, so too is it important
that standards are not escalated or distorted by
unprofessional or unauthorised staff practices.

Work

A.38 The work programme is designed to be hard and
physically demanding and rigorous in content,
being based on conventional manual work -
labouring, farmwork, weaving and necessary
domestic chores. Work and activities in the open
air will continue to take place in most weather
conditions. There will be no change in the
existing earnings scheme.

Education and PE

A.39 There will continue to be a programme of
full-time education for those of school age, part-
time education during the day for those in real
need of remedial education, and a programme of
evening education for all trainees. The content
will be demanding and class teachers will be
expected to require the same high standards of
behaviour as pertain in the regime as a whole.

A.40 The PE programme is to be increased. It is
to continue along existing lines in the main
although some external activities are to be
curtailed.

Health

A.41 Members of staff are reminded that they
should bring to the attention of the hospital
staff, for the information of the medical officer,

any circumstances which give rise to concern about the physical or mental health of any trainee.

Through-care preparation for release

A.42 Probation officers will continue to be seconded to the centres. It is considered important that all staff should maintain a personal interest in individuals, and encourage trainees to seek counsel, advice and support so as to make maximum constructive use of their period in custody.

TOUGHER REGIMES PILOT PROJECT IN TWO DETENTION
CENTRES

NOTE OF GUIDANCE TO STAFF

EVALUATION PROGRAMME

Characteristics of the population

A.43 A study by the Young Offender Psychology Unit
of the Prison Department of the types of offender
received at New Hall and Send, compared with the
inmates of four other detention centres as well as
with those of all six centres (ie including New
Hall and Send) in 1979. This involves taking
samples of the population at each centre,
identifying characteristics such as current
offence, previous offending history and age. This
study has two main purposes: to establish whether
the courts are continuing to send the same type of
offender to New Hall and Send and to enable
allowances to be made for any innate differences
in the population when comparing the results
emerging from other studies.

Characteristics and operation of the regime

A.44 A description of the operation of the regimes
at New Hall and Send and, for comparative
purposes, the regimes of six detention centres
(including New Hall and Send) before the pilot
project was announced as well as the four other
detention centres contemporaneously with the
project itself. This study is being carried out
by the Young Offender Psychology Unit by means of
direct observation supplemented by measurement of
the intensity and frequency of activities as well
as questionnaires addressed to staff and inmates.

269

Its purpose is to record what a tougher regime consists of in practice, including whether it accords with administrators' perceptions, and how it compares with other detention centre regimes.

Effect on inmates attitudes

A.45 A study by the Young Offenders Psychology Unit of the effect of the regime on inmates during their period in custody, primarily by means of questionnaires addressed to samples of them at different stages of sentence and (subject to discussions with the supervising services) during the period of supervision after release. The Unit will also monitor phenomena such as inmate disturbances, absconds and staff sickness rates.

A.46 To examine whether the regime has any more lasting effects, a study will be made of the reconviction rates of offenders who pass through New Hall and Send and, for comparative purposes, four other detention centres. Reconviction rates will however have to be treated with caution. First, because they do not necessarily indicate the effect of custodial regimes as distinct from the many other experiences to which ex-offenders are subject. Secondly, because there may be innate differences in the intakes of different establishments (see A.43 above). If so, the comparisons will be made between similar samples of inmates. The study will examine both general reconviction rates and those associated with sub-groups identified by reference to characteristics such as type of offence, length of criminal record, previous custodial history and age.

Effects on potential offenders

A.47 The Home Office Statistical Department will monitor offence patterns in those police areas which fall within the committal areas of New Hall and Send, to see whether there are any variations over time or from patterns in other areas which can be attributed to the existence of the pilot project.

Response of the courts

A.48 The Home Office Statistical Department will monitor any change in sentencing patterns in the committal areas concerned.

REFERENCES

Bailey, W. 1966. Correctional outcome: An evaluation of 100 reports. Journal of Criminal Law, Criminology and Police Science, 57, pp 153-160.

Baron, R. A. and Ransberger V. M. 1978. Ambient temperature and the occurrence of collective violence: The long hot summer revisited. Journal of Personality and Social Psychology, 36, 4, pp 351-360.

Beyleveld, D. 1978. The effectiveness of general deterrents against crime: An annotated bibliography of evaluative research. Cambridge, University of Cambridge: Institute of Criminology (Microfische).

Brody, S. 1976. The effectiveness of sentencing: A review of the literature. London: HMSO.

Clarke, R. V. G. and Martin, D. N. 1971. Absconding from approved schools. London: HMSO.

Davies, M. B. 1967. The use of the Jesness Inventory on a sample of British probationers. London: HMSO.

Dunlop, A and McCabe, S 1965. Young men in detention centres. London: Routledge.

Elvy, V. 1952. Unpublished paper used as a basis for talks on the first detention centre at Campsfield House.

Everitt, B. S. 1974. Cluster Analysis. London: Heinemann.

Eysenck, H. J. and Eysenck, S. B. 1975. The EPQ.
    London: Hodder and Stroughton.

Eysenck, S. B. and McGurk, B. J. 1980.
    Impulsiveness and venturesomeness in a
    detention centre. Psychological reports, 7,
    pp 1299-1306.

Fisher, R. M. 1967. Acquiescent response, the
    Jesness Inventory and implications for use of
    foreign psychological tests. British Journal
    of Social and Clinical Psychology, 6,
    pp 1-10.

Fludger, N. L. 1976. A comparison of young
    prisoners serving six months or less with
    senior detention centre trainees.
    Unpublished report.

Fludger, N. L. 1977. A survey of the
    characteristics of junior detention centre
    trainees whose home areas are in the prison
    department south-west region or adjoining
    counties. Unpublished report.

Folkard, M. S., Smith, D. E. and Smith, D. D.
    1976. IMPACT: intensive matched probation
    and aftercare treatment. Vol. II. The results
    of the experiment. London: HMSO.

Fowles, A. J. 1978. Prison welfare: an account of
    an experiment at Liverpool. London: HMSO.

Fox, L. 1952. The English Prison and Borstal
    system. London, England: Routledge and Kegan
    Paul.

Friends Home Service Committee, 1968. Detention
    Centres: A report by the sub-committee of the
    friends penal affairs committee: England:
    Henry Burt and Sons.

273

Fuller, J. R. 1980. Personal communication.

Fuller, J. R. and Reynolds, C. 1978. Coerce, coax
    or contain? A study of detention centres and
    their impact. Unpublished report.

Gibbs, J. P. 1975. Crime, punishment and
    deterrence. New York, Elsevier.

Grunhut, M. 1955. Juvenile delinquents under
    punitive detention. British Journal of
    Delinquency, 5, pp 191-209.

Home Office. 1970. Detention Centres. Report of
    the Advisory Council of the Penal System.
    London: HMSO.

Home Office. 1978. The Sentence of the Court.
    London: HMSO.

Home Office. 1952-62. Reports of Commissioners of
    Prisons. London: HMSO.

Home Office. Prisons and Borstals 1963.
    Statistical Tables. Cmnd. 2630. London:
    HMSO.

Home Office. 1964-82. Reports on the work of the
    Prison Department. Statistical Tables.
    London: HMSO.

Hough, M. and Mayhew, P. 1983. The British crime
    survey: first report. London: HMSO.

House of Commons. 1947. Official report (Commons)
    1947. Vol 444, column 2138. London: HMSO.

House of Commons. 1967. Eleventh report from the
    House of Commons estimates committee: session
    1966-1967. London: HMSO.

Jesness, C. F. 1966. Manual of the Jesness
    Inventory. Palo Alto, California:
    Consulting Psychologists Press.

Land, H. 1975. Detention Centres: The experiment
    which could not fail. In Hall, P., Laid, H.,
    Parker, R. and Webb, A. Change Choice and
    Conflict in Social Policy. London:
    Heinemann.

Lipton, D., Martinson, R. and Wilks, J. 1975. The
    effectiveness of correctional treatment. A
    survey of treatment evaluation studies. New
    York: Praeger.

McEwan, A. W. 1981. Could detention centres
    deter? The self reported experience of
    trainees at different stages of their
    sentence. Unpublished report.

Moos, R. H. 1975. Evaluating correctional and
    community settings. New York: John Wiley and
    Sons Inc.

Mott, J. 1969. The Jesness Inventory.
    Applications to approved school boys.
    London: HMSO.

Pigeon, H. 1960. The National Survey Instrument
    6. Windsor, Berks: NFER.

Quay, H. C. 1977. The three faces of evaluation:
    What can be expected to work. Criminal
    Justice and Behaviour, 4, pp 341-354.

Rutter, M. and Giller, H. 1983. Juvenile
    delinquency, trends and perspectives.
    England: Penguin.

SAS Institute Inc. 1982. SAS users' guide:
    statistics 1982 Edition. Cary, N. C.: SAS
    Institute Inc.

Saunders, G. R. and Davies, M. B. 1976. The
    validity of the Jesness Inventory with
    British delinquents. British Journal of
    Social and Clinical Psychology, 15, pp 33-39.

Shapland, P. H. 1969. Detention centre research -
    A pilot study at Whatton Detention Centre.
    Home Office Prison Department. Directorate
    of Psychological Services. C. P. Report 24.

Shaw, M. 1974. Social work in prisons. An
    experiment in the use of extended contact
    with offenders. London: HMSO.

Simon, F. H. 1971. Prediction methods in
    criminology including a prediction study of
    young men on probation. London: HMSO.

Sinclair, I. 1975. The influence of wardens and
    matrons on probation hostels: a study of a
    quasi-family institution. In Tizard, J,
    Sinclair, I. and Clarke, R. V. G. (eds)
    Varieties of residential experience. Great
    Britain: Routledge and Kegan Paul.

Sinclair, I. A. C. and Clark, R. V. G. 1982.
    Predicting, treating and explaining
    delinquency. The lesson from research on
    institutions. In Feldman, M. P. (ed) The
    prevention and control of offending.
    Chichester, England: Wiley.

Thornton, D. and Kline, P. 1982. Reliability and
    validity of the belief in human benevolence
    scale. British Journal of Social Psychology,
    21, pp 57-62.

Watts, A. F. 1948. The Holburn Reading Scale.
    London: Harrap.

Waylen, J. H. 1962. Detention. Prison Service
    Journal Vol. I No. 4.

Weschler, D. 1955. Manual for the Weschler Adult
    Intelligence Scale. New York: The
    Psychology Corporation.

Printed in the UK for HMSO
Dd737903 C25 7/84 10170 (1608)